How  Fought the War

A VIEW FROM THE INSIDE

by Major General Perry M. Smith

U.S. Air Force, Retired
CNN Military Analyst

A BIRCH LANE PRESS BOOK
Published by Carol Publishing Group

A Birch Lane Press Book
Published by Carol Publishing Group

Editorial Offices: 600 Madison Avenue, New York, N.Y. 10022
Sales & Distribution Offices: 120 Enterprise Avenue, Secaucus, N.J. 07094
In Canada: Musson Book Company, a division of General Publishing
   Company, Ltd., Don Mills, Ontario M3B 2T6

Queries regarding rights and permissions should be addressed to Carol
Publishing Group, 600 Madison Avenue, New York, N.Y. 10022

Carol Publishing Group books are available at special discounts for bulk
purchases, for sales promotions, fund raising, or educational purposes.
Special editions can be created to specifications. For details contact:
Special Sales Department, Carol Publishing Group, 120 Enterprise Avenue,
Secaucus, N.J. 07094

Manufactured in the United States of America
10 9 8 7 6 5 4 3 2 1

Library of Congress Cataloging-in-Publication Data

Smith, Perry M. (Perry McCoy)
    How CNN fought the war : a view from the inside / by Perry M.
Smith.
       p. cm.
    "A Birch Lane Press book."
    ISBN 1-55972-090-5 (paper) : ISBN 1-55972-083-2 (cloth)
       1. Cable News Network. 2. Television broadcasting of news—United
    States—History—20th century. 3. Foreign news—United States—
    History—20th century. 4. Persian Gulf War, 1991—Journalists.
    5. Public opinion—United States—History—20th century. 6. Iraq—
    Foreign public opinion, American—History—20th century. 7. War in
    the press—United States—History—20th century. I. Title.
PN4888.T4S64   1991
070.4'499567043—dc20   91-25990
                                                             CIP

How CNN Fought the War

To CONNOR DYESS SMITH
who so lovingly kept me on an even keel
as I quickly went from a life of relative obscurity
to one of instant, albeit fleeting, fame

Contents

Author to Reader

Once in a great while an event takes place that accelerates time, that dramatically changes the course of history. If history is changed, it is changed forever, and multiple paradigm shifts result. Beginning on January 16, 1991, and continuing for the next six weeks, such an event took place. The Gulf War of 1991, or what historians may call the Six-Week War, changed how wars will be fought and the role technology will play in warfare. These six weeks also changed the way the media will cover major international crises and wars.

This book is an attempt by someone who was at the nerve center of CNN in Atlanta from start to finish to explain from a first-hand perspective how CNN dealt with this war. But I must caution the reader. I had not worked for CNN before the war, nor had I any loyalties toward or strong feelings about it. In fact, I had watched CNN only occasionally. If someone had asked me in early January 1991 to identify the anchors on

CNN or on Headline News, I would have been able to come up with a single name, Bernard Shaw.

CNN asked me to comment on events in the Gulf beginning the afternoon of January 14, 1991. On February 28, the day after the war was over, I ended my relationship with CNN and drove home to Augusta, Georgia. So I am, in many ways, an outsider who spent six intense weeks on the inside in Atlanta, where CNN's corporate headquarters and central studio are located. I hope that this unique perspective, and the absence of any long-term relationship with CNN, has helped me to be objective and fair-minded in the analysis and commentary that follow. Also, I should point out that I am writing for the general reader, not for experienced government officials or military experts.

What this book tries to describe is journalism at "warp" speed. It is about reporting fast-moving events directly, quickly, and as accurately as possible within terribly tight time constraints. It is also a story of great controversy, of how during wartime from the enemy capital, live TV reports (via satellites) were made. Though these reports were heavily censored by the enemy government, the various TV networks strongly desired live coverage out of Baghdad, Kuwait City, and other enemy-controlled locations in Iraq and Kuwait. The controversy centered on the fact that vast number of viewers felt that the reports coming out of Baghdad were no more than Iraqi propaganda with a strong anti-American and anti-Coalition flavor. For much of the war, these live TV reports originated only with CNN. The anger over CNN's allowing itself to be used by "this monster" Saddam Hussein was reflected in thousands of phone calls, fax messages, and letters to the news network's headquarters in Atlanta and to its other studios. Hence, this is a story of the profound emotions, conflicting opinions, and trauma of reporters, military analysts, staff members, and viewers.

This is also a story of the people of CNN: committed, hardworking, bright, intense, attractive, imperfect. They lived and worked for six weeks on adrenalin, snacks, and coffee. On the CNN staff, and particularly among its producers, we find extraordinary energy, remarkable decisiveness, and an all-consuming drive and passion to get the story out and get it out *fast*. At CNN, this was the "No-Sleep War" or the "Sleep-Debt War" or the "Sleep-Is-Last-Priority War."

At times 40 million people in the United States were watching CNN. As large as it seems, this number is quite small when compared to the international audience. During the most exciting periods of the conflict hundreds of millions of people watched CNN. In fact, its public relations office estimated the total number of people who watched the network sometime during the war at one billion people in one hundred and eight nations. That is four times the population of the United States. In Brazil alone, 100 million people watched Cable News Network. Of course, not all of the viewers around the globe understood English, but to a considerable extent the pictures told the story.

The use of two full-time military analysts by CNN, and the war commentary we presented, constitutes an interesting and perhaps unique story. As international events relating to the crisis in the Persian Gulf heated up in the late fall of 1990, the executives and staff of CNN gradually concluded that war would probably come. And when it came, in the crisis-covering tradition of CNN, it would be covered on a twenty-four-hour basis from the start of hostilities to finish. Consequently, the leaders of CNN fully understood military analysts would be needed.

CNN had the ground campaign nicely covered. The CNN military analyst, Harry Summers, was a retired army colonel who became well known in the 1970s for a book on the flawed strategy of the Vietnam War. Summers provided useful analysis for CNN from early August 1990, when CNN hired him, until early January 1991, when he left to join another television network. A whole range of people volunteered their services as military experts to CNN. Some were quite obscure; others had impressive records as soldiers and scholars; and a few were quite famous. The booking office in Atlanta even got a call from someone on Oliver North's staff, asking whether CNN might be interested in his services.

After considerable research, CNN selected James Blackwell, of the Center for Strategic and International Studies (CSIS), to replace Summers. For years, CNN had called upon CSIS for military, strategic, and regional analysts. CSIS had been nurtured through the years by David Abshire, a West Point graduate (Class of 1951) who served as US ambassador to the North Atlantic Treaty Organization during the Reagan administration. He had powerful connections within the executive branch of government and the US Congress. Abshire and his vice presidents had recruited a staff of first-rate scholars, including many who had strong military backgrounds.

James Blackwell, a West Point graduate (Class of 1974) and a man of considerable military experience with the US Army, had retired for medical reasons with the rank of major. He also had a fine educational background, including a Ph.D. from Tufts University and he had taught in the highly respected Social Sciences Department at West Point. Staffers at CNN in Washington and Atlanta were glad to have as Harry Summers's replacement someone as bright and engaging and easy to work with as James Blackwell, even though Blackwell was less experienced in military affairs and had not served in combat.

Geography influenced the selection of Blackwell to some extent. The CNN studio in Washington had maps and other visual aids for use in explaining military affairs, and it made sense for the CNN military analyst to be located there. Washington also gave easy access to the Pentagon, another reason for locating the CNN military analyst there.

On the air combat side, however, CNN had a gap. To CNN executives it seemed likely that combat would commence with heavy air activity, for most of the military preparation seemed to be pointing in that direction. Gail Evans, CNN vice president for network booking, decided to approach Gen. Michael Dugan, the former chief of staff of the United States Air Force, for an interview. Evans had in mind the possibility of offering him a job as the second military analyst if he interviewed well and was willing to join CNN for the duration of the war. But Evans had some reservations. Dugan was controversial. He had been fired on September 17, 1990, by Secretary of Defense Dick Cheney for revealing to the press the outline of the upcoming air campaign and for predicting the predominance of air power and seeming to denigrate the role of the ground forces.

When asked by W. Thomas Johnson, Jr., the president of CNN, to do an interview, Dugan was reluctant, because he had been alerted by Gail Evans that one of the questions would have to be "Why were you fired?"

Johnson then told Dugan he was looking for an airman to cover the upcoming war and asked for Dugan's advice. The man to get, Dugan suggested, was "Perry Smith, who lives down there in Atlanta." Dugan knew I had recently moved from Virginia to Georgia, but he thought, incorrectly, that I had moved to Atlanta. In fact, I had moved to Augusta, a city 150 miles to the east. Dugan and I had served together at the Air Force Academy and later in the Pentagon, and he was familiar with my books on leadership and on the Pentagon. In addition, we had written to each other a few times about how the air force might do a better job of providing visionary leadership to the nation. As fellow West Pointers, fighter pilots, and air force general officers, we had much in common.

Judy Stewart, a member of Evans's CNN staff, frantically began searching for me in Atlanta and finally found me at my new home in Augusta on the Friday before the war started. I was invited to do an interview on the following Monday, January 14. After accepting the invitation, I called two former colleagues who held key jobs in the Pentagon. Both gave me indications that war was imminent. The interview seemed to go well. Asked on the air by CNN anchor Lou Waters when I expected the war to commence, I suggested, "Within the next four days."

After this short interview, I returned to Gail Evans's office on the sixth floor, where she offered me the opportunity to become part of the CNN team for the duration of the war. When I asked about the financial arrangements, she told me I would be given a room at the Omni Hotel, adjacent to the CNN studio, and that all my expenses would be paid, but there would be no other compensation. CNN would lose a great deal of money during the war, she said, and so could not afford to pay a second military analyst. I told her I would think about this offer, then drove back to Augusta. In late January, February, and March, I had a number of speaking engagements, and I was working on a new book. I did not feel it was fair to devote many weeks of my time to assisting CNN without some compensation. Still, I was tempted, since it was clear that CNN needed help and sincerely wanted my assistance. It seemed the job might be an extraordinarily challenging experience as well.

Two days later, the war began, as expected, with a massive air campaign. I called Evans. "Do you still want me?" I asked. Very much, she indicated, and asked me to drive to Atlanta right away. I would be placed at the anchor desk, she said, soon after I arrived.

I talked the matter over with Connor, my wife of thirty-one years. I could be gone for many weeks. She asked me if I wanted to work as an analyst, and I said, "Yes." She suggested that I take the job, since she felt I could make a contribution. So, a few minutes later, I called Evans back. "I am on my way," I said. She replied, "Wonderful! Please come quickly."

Just a few minutes earlier, there had been great excitement at CNN. At 6:35 PM David French, the handsome and calm CNN anchor on camera in the Washington studio, had just started to interview Caspar Weinberger, the former secretary of defense who was responsible for the large American defense buildup during the Reagan administration. French had just asked, "How inevitable tonight is battle?" and Weinberger had replied, "He [Saddam Hussein] doesn't seem to want anything but war. If that is what he wants, he will get it." French started to ask the next question, but appeared to be distracted for a couple of seconds. He then said, "We have to go to Baghdad, Secretary." Bernard Shaw then came on the air (by telephone). Shaw said, "This is, ah... Something is happening outside."

CNN coverage of the Gulf War had begun and it continued without stop for nine hundred hours.

That evening I drove to Atlanta faster than I had driven since I last navigated the no-speed-limit autobahns of Germany. As I drove across the state, I listened to various radio stations. National Public Radio seemed to me to have the best coverage. I was trying hard to figure out what was going on in those first hours of the war. About fifty miles short of Atlanta, I had to stop for gas; just before I pulled into the gas station, I said to myself, "You know, Perry, you really don't know much. You'd better talk to someone who does."

So I picked up the phone at a local motel and tried to locate a close friend at the Pentagon. He and I had talked in the previous months about the likelihood of war and how it might be conducted. I had great respect for his intellect, and he was very well informed. I trusted him. Perhaps more important, he trusted me. When I got no answer at his regular Pentagon number, I called his wife, who gave me his new number and his portable phone number. I reached him immediately and said that I was going to work for CNN as a quasi journalist. What I most needed before I walked into the CNN Atlanta studio, I explained, was some unclassified background information.

He was very helpful. He said he would tell me what he could. He then gave me a twenty-minute rundown on the basic strategy of the war, the tactics, what had been accomplished that evening and what might be expected during the next day or two. He separated the information that I could use on the air from what I could not. I warmly thanked him, hung up, and raced off to downtown Atlanta. During the final hour of my drive, I practiced out loud the answers to the questions I expected I might get. I was glad it was dark. Otherwise, drivers on Interstate 20 might have thought the fellow talking to himself as he drove down the highway was a crazy old geezer.

A few minutes before midnight I arrived at the Omni Hotel. As soon as I walked in, the man at reception asked if I was General Smith. In urgent tones he told me that I was wanted at CNN—"right now"—and volunteered to check me in. I dropped my bags and jogged over to the CNN studio, a block away.

There was telephone commentary coming out of Baghdad. Bernard Shaw, Peter Arnett, and John Holliman were reporting heavy antiaircraft artillery fire, and large explosions at ground level. This confirmed some of the things that I had learned from my Pentagon friend. Within a few minutes I was at the anchor desk for a live interview with Patrick Greenlaw. In very rapid order he asked me numerous questions about what was going on.

These challenging questions from Greenlaw started me on an extraordinary six weeks of sixteen-, eighteen-, and—in a few cases—twenty-hour days. When I wasn't on the air, I found myself on the telephone to the Pentagon, to the war colleges, and to various friends and acquaintances, trying to gain an understanding of the short- and long-term implications of the combat activity on both sides. To provide objective analysis, I needed help. Dozens of people went out of their way to answer my questions, undertake research for me, and react to my ideas. Many of those who helped me watched CNN and heard their ideas coming from my mouth within a few minutes of talking to me. I am in debt to them.

What follows is my story of the war as seen from CNN, Atlanta. I started to write it before the war was over, and I finished it four months after the liberation of Kuwait. The advantage of writing the book so quickly is that events were fresh in my mind and in the minds of those I interviewed for the book. The disadvantage is that I have not allowed myself the luxury of time and hence have not had the benefit of fuller and more deliberate research.

How CNN Fought the War

The First Night and Its Aftermath

I have been welcomed memorably many times in my life. On December 7, 1941, at the age of six, I experienced a wild ride in an Army truck with my older sister and a bunch of other army brats as we returned from Sunday School to my home in Honolulu, Hawaii. My mother and my grandmother, who had sent us off to church that morning, before the Japanese attack began, were relieved beyond description when they realized we had survived and were safe. We were not a family that did a lot of hugging, but there was hugging all around that Sunday morning. Many years later, in August 1969, I was warmly welcomed back by my wife and two small children from a year of combat.

More recently, my wife and I were welcomed by family and friends in the city of Augusta, Georgia, when we moved there in 1990 to live out the rest of our lives. There have been many other times that I have been welcomed in the forty times I have picked up, packed up, and moved to a new location. Life as an army brat (the son of an army officer) and later as an air force officer was full of farewells and welcomes.

But I received one of my warmest welcomes ever when I walked into the CNN studio shortly after midnight, the night the war began. The producers, bookers, anchors, and staffers had been waiting for me impatiently. They felt they needed my analysis, particularly of the air campaign that had started in its full fury that night. I was quickly seated at the anchor desk, provided makeup on the spot, and launched into my first wartime television interview—at 12:18 AM on January 17, 1991.

There seemed to be no time for anyone to so much as whisper to me the first of the many questions I was to be asked. I was on my own in my initial commentary, which was watched live throughout the world. Remember, now, it is the first night of the war, eighteen minutes after midnight, and I have spent the hours since the war began (about 6:35 PM Eastern Standard Time) at a mad pace—grabbing a quick supper, doing an interview in my home for local television (Channel 6, WJBF Augusta), packing my bags, watching the President's 9:00 PM address to the nation and driving from Augusta to Atlanta. But, remember, too, I had had that telephone conversation with my friend in the Pentagon on the way to the studio. That telephone call was probably the most fruitful call I had made in the last ten years.

In rapid order, CNN anchor Patrick Greenlaw asked me eleven questions. Let me summarize this question-and-answer period. Greenlaw wanted to know how the coalition had managed to do so well. I replied that the aircraft came in low, jammed the enemy radars, used some newly developed tactics, and overwhelmed the Iraqi air defense system. Asked if I was surprised at the success, I replied, "I am not really surprised, because we had so much time to practice. We have such good systems, and we have such a massive amount of air."

Asked what aircraft were used, I identified the Stealth fighter (F-117), the F-15E, and the F-111. When Greenlaw asked what to expect next, I suggested that there would be more attacks in the Baghdad area and then a shift to Kuwait to hit Iraqi forces there. Greenlaw then posed an important question about the decisiveness of air power and the use of ground forces in "a mopping-up kind of operation." Here is my complete answer.

SMITH: This is a *very* important point. We see a major doctrinal shift here; and that is, that in all times in history when we had massed armies face each other with air power, air power was always in support of the massed army. Now, we have the air forces in the lead, perhaps even decisively in the lead, with the army and ground forces more in a supporting role. The situation is ideal. You have a desert situation. You have had plenty of time for training. You have a very massive amount of air power, but it may be a unique time in history where, in a tactical situation, air power would be the decisive element."

In answer to other questions from Greenlaw, I made the point that we had learned many lessons from the Vietnam War and developed better training, greater accuracy, better technology, and better cooperation among the services. I stressed that we could expect better bombing accuracies than in previous wars, especially with precision-guided bombs.

As I look back on this first wartime interview, I see that Greenlaw had very good questions. Within a few hours of the start of the war, he was asking about a mopping-up operation on the ground rather than talking about a lengthy ground campaign. I also see I made many errors that first night, although, happily, most of them were small. (I have reviewed the vast majority of my appearances on CNN, and in a later chapter I will describe my biggest mistakes.) I had to react quickly to events, with little time for research. It was crystal clear on the first night of the Gulf War that the careful research techniques I had learned at Columbia University would not and could not apply.

Having arrived at the anchor desk in the early morning hours of January 17, it seemed quite natural for me to stay in the studio to observe the activities and be ready to react to further events. Around three o'clock someone suggested that I try to catch some sleep, so I went to my room in the Omni Hotel. But there I turned on CNN and just couldn't keep my eyes off the screen. Like many viewers, I was so wrapped up in what was happening, so interested in what was going to happen next, and so caught up in all the reports coming in, that I could not fall asleep. This, I found, was true of almost everybody at CNN. Around the world, CNN employees quickly went into sleep deficit, not just because there was so much to do in the wee hours of the morning, but because it was impossible not to feel the excitement.

It would be hard to overemphasize how important the first days of the war were to CNN, to the future of twenty-four-hour reporting in times of crisis and combat, and, in a less happy way, to the other American networks, especially ABC, CBS, and NBC.

As *Entertainment Weekly* magazine pointed out in its February 1 issue, "Within minutes of the first bomb burst over Baghdad, the Cable News Network achieved total air superiority over the networks and held it until Iraq temporarily shut down the news operations some sixteen hours later. Ten-year-old CNN, the news organization once derided as the chicken noodle network, ordinarily scores less than one-tenth the ratings of competitors ABC, CBS, and NBC. But on January 16, the first day of the war, 10.8 million households tuned in to CNN, only 1.6 million short of CBS's score. Actually CNN had an even bigger audience than the reported numbers, because hundreds of stations around the country carried its coverage, including many affiliates who switched from their own networks to feed to CNN's. As Dick Aiken of Britain's ITV Channel put it, 'They cut to Bernie Shaw [CNN's anchor in Iraq] because it was clear that they were getting their heads handed to them.'"

The activity level in the CNN studio in Atlanta during this first day or two was awesome. There was much to be done. First, it was important that CNN continue to have live telephone coverage from Baghdad, while working hard to get live television coverage. CNN also wanted live television coverage from other key places in the Middle East, as well as new stories, insights, perspectives, and points of view in order to inform and to hold the audience. CNN needed to obtain help from independent contractors and consultants in order to sustain and hold public interest. One of the most innovative actions of this first day or two was the rapid hiring of lots of people, some for a few days and some for the duration of the war. There was a full realization at every level in CNN that this was the time to act dynamically, to move quickly, to rapidly turn an idea into an on-the-air production, not just to beat the competition but to blow it away.

The activity level of the two men responsible for production, the frenetic Bob Furnad and the more placid Paul Amos, was interesting to watch. The tension was palpable, like electricity racing around that studio. Each night, I found it almost impossible to return to my hotel to sleep. Of all the places to be in America to watch the war unfold, the best was the CNN studio in Atlanta. History was being made, and people wanted to be there to report it.

As early as the second day, there was an air of congratulation, because the folks of CNN knew that the network was doing well. But it was self-congratulation based on the judgment that the work they were performing was first-rate and that the beats they were getting were legitimate. It wasn't just the generation of stories, but the handling of these stories in a balanced way that provided most of the satisfaction.

As the war rolled on, CNN received a great deal of criticism from some quarters for having much coverage but very little analysis. That criticism was well founded during the first couple of days. However, the CNN leadership was aware of this weakness and soon began looking for ways to provide more and better analysis. By about the third day, a range of solid analysis was coming through.

Throughout the war CNN provided more analysis than the other networks. Bill Moyers provided broad strategic perspectives. Over sixty military experts provided views that went well beyond instant reaction to breaking events. Former officials in the Department of Defense, like Richard Perle and Francis "Bing" West, provided thoughtful analysis and perspectives. The "Gulf Talk" show, hosted by Bernard Shaw and featuring such guests as former Secretary of State Henry Kissinger, aired daily at 11:00 PM; it was basically a half hour of analysis. James Blackwell and I tried hard to provide more than just instant reaction to events; in fact, one of our goals was to grab as much camera time as we could to make available thorough, continual analysis. For instance, I wrote and delivered perspectives on combat leadership, civilian casualties of warfare, and myths and realities of the Gulf War; I recommended books, magazines, and newspapers; and I discussed leadership, empowerment, and integrity.

For many years to come, journalists will study the first few days of the Gulf War and ask how CNN succeeded so well. The answer is quite simple. CNN was ready. It was accomplished in providing twenty-four-hour coverage. The cable network had been doing this for over ten years, getting better and better at it with each passing year. CNN had the reporters, the satellite linkups, the engineers, the producers, and expert commentators in place or on standby. It had a leadership team which understood, before the war broke out, that this was going to be a story of giant proportions. They knew this war would provide an extraordinary opportunity for CNN to show its stuff to the world. CNN also possessed an innovative spirit. It was ready to spend money, to take risks, to try new things. (Speaking of spending money, I suggested on about the third night of the war—and after two major networks had contacted me about providing analysis of the air campaign—that CNN might wish to provide me with some "modest compensation" for my services. A quick decision was made and my request was granted.)

The kind of innovation that CNN undertook early in the war can be seen from two examples. Someone suggested that the two military analysts be given telestrators (we called them the John Madden machines) to better describe the gun camera and strike camera film. James Blackwell and I each received one, got checked out quickly on the technique, and were using them on camera in less than a day's time. Someone else heard about a person who was an animator who could perform magic on a Macintosh computer. He was hired in an instant, and the moment he arrived from California he began working through the night to provide animation illustrating military systems at work. Receptivity to innovation and the velocity of decision making were two keys to CNN's coverage, particularly in those first few crucial days when viewers were deciding which network they would watch.

Throughout the war the work hours of the people at CNN, from the top producers all the way down to the staffers, were quite long. On average, they worked between ten and twelve hours a day, and in some cases fourteen and sixteen hours. They got about one day off each week, although many worked the first eighteen days without a single day off. Of course, they were very interested in their work, and caught up in the intensity of the operation. They felt, and rightly so, that they were needed to support the operation, and so they worked very long hours without much complaint. The fact that the bosses were also working these very long hours, and were present and willing to listen to their ideas and complaints, made duty at CNN during this extraordinary period more a pleasure than a burden, more a privilege than an imposition.

The first day of the war deeply affected the lives of CNN employees around the world. January 16 was also the date of a momentous decision by Tom Johnson, the CNN president. In an interview with Johnson in his office three weeks after Kuwait was liberated, I asked him what gave him the greatest agony during the war. Johnson said that without question it was an event that took place on the afternoon of January 16.

Johnson received a call from Marlin Fitzwater, the White House press spokesman, recommending, on behalf of President George Bush, that the CNN team in Baghdad be pulled out immediately. Fitzwater said that Baghdad was going to be very dangerous for the CNN team and their lives would soon be in grave danger. The CNN team in Baghdad consisted of three reporters, Bernie Shaw, John Holliman, and Peter Arnett, as well as a small group of cameramen, engineers, and other support personnel. Johnson faced a tough decision, and he had to make it fast.

In early January, Johnson had contracted for a jet at Amman, Jordan, at $10,000 per day. It was prepared to zip into Baghdad and get his whole team out on very short notice, if necessary. Hence, he had a way to pull them out fast. After the telephone call from the White House, Johnson and his boss, Ted Turner, discussed the matter and decided that those who wanted to leave Baghdad could do so and those who wanted to stay could remain. All three correspondents, as well as the rest of the CNN team, elected to stay, with the full understanding that they might be facing considerable risks.

As the publisher of the *Los Angeles Times* Johnson had seen two of his reporters killed, one in Teheran during the overthrow of the shah and another in Nicaragua during the civil war there. He knew what it was like to have employees who were also friends put their lives at risk in dangerous situations.

Johnson experienced one more agonizing moment during the early days of the Gulf War. On the second day, a call from NBC indicated the Rashid Hotel was going to be bombed by Coalition aircraft that night.

The CNN team in Baghdad might be in grave danger. Johnson called Gen. Colin Powell, chairman of the Joint Chiefs of Staff, in the Pentagon and told him that he knew he was way out of bounds in raising this issue, but was it true that the Rashid Hotel was about to be bombed? Powell was incensed. The hotel was filled with civilians, including one of Powell's close friends, Bernie Shaw. How could Johnson think such a thing? This was not one of the most pleasant conversations Johnson had during the war, but it greatly eased his concerns. The Rashid Hotel was never bombed.

The CNN Background

In order to grasp the impact that CNN made in capturing the attention of the world, it is essential to understand a bit of the CNN background and how it got to where it was when the Gulf War started. CNN was the dream of Ted Turner, who wanted to form a twenty-four-hour cable news network. Despite the great skepticism of many people, he assembled a competent team in the late 1970s and launched CNN in 1980. It got off to a rocky start. A multitude of mistakes were made trying to maintain twenty-four-hour news coverage and keep it fresh and interesting. CNN thus received mixed reviews, at best, during the early years. More recently, the staff had grown and improved, the satellite hookups had increased, and the numbers and talents of people in Atlanta, Washington, and out in the field had become somewhat more impressive.

The coverage of a number of major crises had put CNN on the map even before the Gulf War. The bombing of the US

Marine Corps barracks in Lebanon in 1983, the *Challenger* space shuttle tragedy in 1985, the heartwarming rescue of Jessica McClure from an abandoned well in west Texas in 1987, and the Tiananmen Square crisis in Beijing in 1989 showed the world how thoroughly CNN could cover major crises and disasters. With each crisis CNN made mistakes, but with each it also became more proficient.

Some of CNN's key reporters and anchors also gained recognition during noncrisis periods. In the presidential campaign of 1988, it was Bernard Shaw of CNN who asked the most devastating question. Right off the bat, in the second debate between Michael Dukakis and George Bush, Shaw asked Dukakis about his views on capital punishment: would they change if his wife, Kitty, were "raped and murdered?" Dukakis's answer, and his cool demeanor as he gave it, drove a nail into the coffin that was his campaign. Later, political experts agreed that by the time Dukakis finished his answer the presidential race was over.

Bernard Shaw also asked George Bush a tough question about whether he would worry about the country if it came under President Dan Quayle should Bush suddenly die. That evening Bernard Shaw became famous throughout the world. The fact that he was a CNN anchor helped build its reputation as a network that asked the kinds of tough questions that were on the minds of so many.

The next major CNN coup took place during the spring and early summer of 1989. The issue then was China. CNN sent Bernard Shaw to Beijing. CBS sent Dan Rather. Peter Jennings of ABC and Tom Brokaw of NBC stayed home. Shaw's purpose in going to China was to cover the visit of Soviet president Mikhail Gorbachev, who for the first time was meeting with senior leaders of the People's Republic of China. In the background during the visit was the burgeoning Democracy movement of Chinese university students. Many had gathered in Tiananmen Square, in the heart of Beijing, to seek a restructuring of Chinese political leadership.

All of a sudden, with the Gorbachev visit coming to an end, the Chinese government threatened to suppress the student movement. CNN had good coverage of the events in Tiananmen Square. In fact, as the Chinese authorities began their crackdown, it had the *only* live coverage, and the Chinese wanted to stop it. These developments, and CNN's efforts to continue coverage from Beijing, became a story in itself. ABC, for instance, began covering the story of CNN's efforts to hang on to its coverage even after the Gorbachev visit ended.

The attention of the world was focused on Tiananmen Square, and CNN was providing extensive coverage, not just to the United States, but to the world. Shaw said, "We all came here to cover a summit and we walked into a revolution." His articulate coverage, plus the satellite feed out of Beijing, again brought CNN to the forefront, gave the network more practice in dealing with crisis situations, and enhanced the prestige of CNN throughout the world. This CNN coup in China and the short but dramatic history of CNN is told quite nicely in the book *CNN: The Inside Story* by Hank Whittemore, published by Little, Brown in 1989.

As the network approached its tenth anniversary on the first of June 1990, it had become one of the success stories of American business. It was being received in fifty-three million American homes by cable and in eighty-four countries. By the time the Gulf War broke out, it was reaching one hundred and eight countries. By 1990 there were seventeen hundred staffers and seventeen bureaus; by 1991 that had grown to eighteen hundred staffers and twenty-four bureaus. Yet in order to understand how these people pulled the news together, it is necessary to examine the technology, the newsgathering and sorting process, and the structure and functioning of the main CNN studio in Atlanta.

One of CNN's biggest strengths is its technical ability to pull together a large amount of information from various places and feed it into the control room in Atlanta. As a result, the producers had a variety of material to choose from, including live and taped shots, live telephone hookups, and military experts in Washington and Atlanta who could be on camera in less than two minutes. With a veritable cornucopia of interesting material at their command, these producers could quickly place a vital story on camera.

In order to turn this juggling act into compelling television, the producers needed a workable but flexible plan. Each day they had to have scripted stories, dozens of guest experts, and a great deal of satellite time (with the up-links and the down-links to and from the satellites well established). Success required decisive producers who could quickly monitor an enormous amount of information and identify and select the best stories.

This diverse menu of choices came about because there were many producers and reporters in the field feeding information to producers in the control room in Atlanta and telling them about present and upcoming stories. A crucial role was also played by highly competent technical people who could say, "Okay, we've got five minutes of satellite time left with Amman," or "We have ten minutes of satellite time coming out of Riyadh at the top of the hour."

Producers needed to grasp not only where the best stories were located but whether they could bring them into Atlanta when the satellite was available. They also had to understand which alternative routes could be used if the satellite up-links or down-links were not working properly.

The control room (often called "A control" or the "pit") in Atlanta is the nerve center (or command post) for the entire operation. In this two-tiered booth are sixty television monitors for technicians, producers, and senior producers to survey. During the war the normal pit crew went from seven to twelve persons so that nothing important was missed, no telephone call went unanswered, and no sharp direction by a producer was ignored. The executive producers could communicate directly to dozens of reporters throughout the world through earpieces and at the same time give directions to anchors and military experts sitting at desks in Atlanta and Washington.

When a producer or executive producer gave a command through an earpiece, the reporter or guest or technician did what he or she was asked, and did it quickly. The hardest job was to talk live on camera while listening to directions from a producer. Usually the producer's directions were cryptic: "Wrap" meant finish your point and quit talking within the next ten or fifteen seconds; "stretch" meant keep talking. "Stretch" usually meant, in fact, that there was an unantici-pated delay with the next story and that it was the reporter's job to keep talking for a while. (I loved it when I heard the word "stretch" through my earpiece, for I always had more to say about the subject at hand.) CNN officials, from top executive to junior technician, had planned for rapid-fire coverage emanating from many locations. The result, on occasion, was chaos, but at times it provided brilliant broadcast journalism.

CNN has an efficient way to keep busy reporters, producers, bookers, anchors, and staff people informed. It is the Basys computer system, an electronic mail system which permits CNN employees to communicate with each other and keep up to date on the thinking of top CNN officials, on events relating to the Gulf War, and on other newsworthy happenings. Throughout CNN there are computer terminals at hundreds of locations. On the central CNN computer during the war were two files of great importance: the "Read Me" file and the "Read Me War" file. Every key employee (reporter, producer, anchor, booker, executive) would go to a computer terminal and call up these files, which provided updates on major issues and policy decisions, when they arrived at work and at least every hour during the day.

Executive Vice President Ed Turner (no relation to Ted Turner) served as chief news gatherer, and he used this system to communicate to his staff around the globe. Using this computer system, CNN employees could call up the major American and European wire services, such as Associated Press, United Press International, Reuters, or Agence France Presse. They could also send and receive private messages to and from anyone else in CNN. Many organizations with which I have been associated in recent years have similar systems, but none uses them as extensively as does CNN. Without question the Basys system was an important part of the CNN success story. Little time was wasted trying to make telephone contact with busy people. "Telephone tag," that frustrating exercise of trying and failing to get someone on the telephone, was largely avoided by CNN throughout the war.

As the result of newly established satellite up-links, CNN had more opportunities to set up guest appearances than had ever been available in the past. For instance, CNN could use London for the first time as a regular base for guests. In the past, getting a live interview with the British prime minister or with the distinguished British military historian John Keegan had required setting up satellite time. Now such interviews became routine.

CNN also had the capacity, for the first time, to conduct regular live interviews with government officials and other experts in Tel Aviv and Jerusalem, Amman and Riyadh. This expanded coverage really paid off when the war broke out. Although the other networks had some fine producers and reporters in the field, they did not have as many people in as many key places, nor did they have enough satellite time to transmit extensive live coverage. There were some heavy economic costs for CNN for such coverage, of course. In fact, CNN spent more money on satellite time during the Gulf War than any of the other networks.

The other networks generally used tapes from overseas locations while CNN often came on live. CNN understood that when people are watching a war, they are interested in getting as much up-to-the-minute information as possible. They want to see the raw stuff, to learn about what's happening *now*. They do not want the kind of analysis that reduces the news to "this is what we think you ought to know about this issue."

In peacetime, most viewers may be quite comfortable with a once-a-day, carefully orchestrated twenty-one-minute presentation that the three major networks provide. But in a war situation, they want to make their own judgments about what they are seeing rather than having the news boiled down and analyzed for them. In this war, the viewers became "news junkies," and in considerable numbers they chose CNN, the network having the largest concentration of professional news junkies in the world.

The viewers were really caught up in what was happening, especially in times of great tension. They tended to forgive CNN when they saw the confusion and the anxiety on camera. When sirens wailed in Tel Aviv, Jerusalem, and Riyadh, reporters had their cameras tied down, sent their camera crews to shelters, and grabbed their gas masks. It might not have been polished television journalism emanating from a fancy studio in New York, but it was very real.

CNN's success also grew out of the fortunate fact that it had designed its control facility in the CNN center in Atlanta, its production and anchor desks, and its news area specifically for crisis situations. CNN executives knew that during crises (aircraft crashes, tornadoes, earthquakes, wars), CNN would attract its peak viewership. As a result, CNN developed a system for handling the most complex crisis in hopes of beating the competition during each and every emergency. As you might expect, this type of studio also proved easy to run on slow news days. Thus CNN executives chose to design a technically first-rate studio ready to accept lots of information, sort it out efficiently, and quickly broadcast it.

The large newsroom is directly behind the anchor desk with a massive window in between that screens out any noise. In this newsroom, which can be seen on camera immediately behind the twin anchors in Atlanta, are a series of three circular working areas. Around the periphery of each circle sit about ten staff writers. In the middle of the circle and sitting above the staff writers so he or she can observe the entire newsroom is a copy editor. This copy editor reads and edits all the copy that is being produced by the staff writers.

Behind these three script-writing areas are the national and international areas. These are also on a higher tier so the supervising producers and other key officials can closely watch the whole news-gathering operation. In one corner of the newsroom is the graphics area, and in the rear are many small booths for reviewing the latest television tape. On the same floor is a small library with tapes from the previous few days. These short tapes are numbered and can be grabbed and put on the air in a minute or two. Although a less chaotic place than the pit, the newsroom was a very busy place during the war. It was quite common to see someone running across the newsroom toward the pit wearing a frantic look.

The booking office is up a flight of stairs and adjacent to the offices of the CNN executives. The main library and the snack bar are immediately downstairs from the newsroom. Every key official in Atlanta is within a one-minute walk of the control room (the pit) which is adjacent to the anchor desk and the newsroom. It is in the pit that everything is pulled together by the producers and the executive producers.

CNN was ready with a substantial staff, a robust system, good satellite linkups, and experience in dealing with many crises on a twenty-four-hour basis. Everything was in place for what would soon become a great media success. The coverage would emanate not only from the Persian Gulf region but from many other locations. In fact, some of the most dramatic CNN coverage would come from Israel.

The euphoria that most viewers experienced during the successful raids of the first night did not last long. By Day Two, the Scud attacks began, and many throughout the world held their breath.

The Scuds and the Patriots

As war approached, Gen. H. Norman Schwarzkopf and his staff were quite confident that Iraqi Scud missiles would not present a major problem. They were dead wrong. Herein is an example of military leaders examining the capability of a weapons system without fully considering its strategic significance. The Scud was an old, obsolete missile, so inaccurate that an impact within a mile or two of a target was about all that the Iraqis could expect. Contempt on the part of the military leaders of the Coalition for such an inaccurate weapons system led to complacency about its potential political and strategic consequences.

But there is much more to this story. Schwarzkopf had been told by his intelligence advisors that the Iraqis had about a thousand Scud missiles but fewer than fifty Scud launchers. He therefore felt that the Scuds would be only a modest problem, since the launchers could be destroyed early in the war and, in the meantime, the Scuds could do little damage to military targets since they were so inaccurate.

Within forty-eight hours of the war's beginning, the Scuds were being launched toward Israel and Saudi Arabia, and Schwarzkopf faced a serious problem. In fact, this is one of the few areas where he got very specific guidance from Secretary of Defense Cheney. This guidance was simple, direct, and very firm. Locate and knock out those Scud launchers quickly and use all necessary resources to do so. Schwarzkopf followed his orders, even though it meant a significant diversion of aircraft and intelligence resources from his carefully planned air campaign. In this area, Schwarzkopf's famed temper came to the surface. How could his intelligence experts be so off the mark as far as the number of Scud launchers available to the Iraqi military? With his great array of intelligence assets, why couldn't we do a better job of counting and finding these launchers?

The failure was not just an intelligence failure. Tactical innovation, which was impressive in the campaign against Iraqi ground forces, came quite slowly in this area. For instance, the United States Space Command was able to give precise firing locations to Schwarzkopf's staff within three minutes of the Scud launch. Yet it took a couple of weeks, including a prod from the Pentagon, before a tactic was devised to put F-15Es on airborne alert so they could quickly receive the targeting information from Space Command and attack the launcher that had just fired a Scud. Once this tactic was devised, the numbers of Scud launchers destroyed each night increased. Nevertheless, the Scuds still fired almost every night and Schwarzkopf's and Cheney's frustration grew. The good news was that the number of Scuds fired slowly but steadily decreased so it became clear that Schwarzkopf was making progress in dealing with the problem.

The problem of Scuds being fired at Saudi Arabia was manageable since US Patriot missile batteries were in place and were intercepting the Scuds with impressive regularity. However, there were two significant problems with the Scud attacks on Saudi Arabia. The Patriot had been designed to shoot down supersonic aircraft, then upgraded to intercept tactical ballistic missiles. This upgrade was a wise decision, but the Patriot was unable to destroy, in every case, the Scud warhead itself. Second, the ground radar in the Patriot system sometimes failed to detect an incoming missile. In Saudi Arabia, an undetected Scud slammed into a military barracks and killed twenty-eight Americans in the explosion of the warhead and in the fire that followed.

The problem of Scud attacks on Israel turned out to be a huge one. The Israelis could not intercept Scuds at all, and the urge of the Israeli military to retaliate against Iraq for these Scud attacks was palpable. Ironically, the Israelis had Patriot missiles, but their crews had not finished their training and, even more important, the Israeli Patriots did not have the upgrade package which would permit them to intercept ballistic missiles like the Scuds. Israelis lay naked before the Scuds of Saddam.

This difficult problem quickly led to one of the masterstrokes of the war. The dilemma for the United States government was how to protect Israel before Israel retaliated against Iraq. The great concern on the part of George Bush and many other Coalition leaders was the damage Israeli military action might have on the fragile Coalition. With the concurrence of the Israeli government, a quick decision was made: The United States would send Patriot missiles from Germany to Israel, and do it speedily. In the meantime, President Bush sent one of America's most skillful diplomats, Lawrence Eagleburger, to figuratively hold the hands of Israeli leaders until the Patriots were in place and fully operational. Within twenty-four hours of their arrival, the Patriots were operational and ready to intercept Scud missiles. Israel did not attack Iraq; the Coalition held together.

After the war was over an article in the *New York Times* raised serious questions about the efficacy of the Patriots in Israel. It argued that if the Patriot missiles had not been sent to Israel, there would have been less damage, since some of the Scud warheads which got through caused quite a bit of damage. However, it seems to me the strategic decision to send Patriots to Israel was correct, irrespective of the fact that it may not be certain that they did an effective job of intercepting Scuds.

The purpose of sending Patriots was to show American

commitment, to try our best to intercept the missiles, and to prevent the Israelis from retaliating. All these goals were achieved. Secretary of Defense Cheney deserves the most credit for initiating and implementing this masterstroke. Other stars of this episode were the Patriot crews themselves and the crews of the C-5 aircraft who moved these missiles from Germany to Israel with such great care and alacrity.

President Bush later made a dramatic visit to the Raytheon factory in Massachusetts where the Patriots are manufactured to thank the workers for their contributions to the war effort. The Strategic Defense Initiative office in the Pentagon also took heart that an American missile could, in fact, intercept incoming ballistic missiles with excellent, albeit imperfect, results. Sophisticated technology, which had worked so well with Stealth fighters and precision-guided bombs, functioned with antimissile missiles. The future course of warfare and deterrence should be altered significantly as a result.

The Press Coverage: The Minuses and the Pluses

Within the first few days of the outbreak of the war, it was evident to most viewers of television that this war was going to be different from previous wars. Well-trained aircrews and high technology systems were already achieving impressive results. One of the more interesting aspects of the press coverage of this war was the slowness some journalists displayed in understanding what was going on.

For fifteen years prior to the outbreak of the war of 1991, many members of the media had written articles or delivered radio or television commentaries that were quite critical of the Department of Defense. Such articles and commentaries tended to criticize the enormous Pentagon bureaucracy. They attacked the slowness of the decision-making process, inter-service and intraservice rivalries, weaknesses in the procurement system, and "gold-plating" of the research and development programs. As to the truth of these accusations—and the reporters certainly uncovered situations deserving change or correction—I am not prepared to argue here. But these reports also discussed the heavy emphasis by the military on high-technology systems that were very sophisticated and supposedly very unreliable. This pattern of criticism led to a rigidity of thinking among these critics: Nothing was going to work the way the military planners and developers said it would work. They became convinced that American military weapons systems were much more expensive than they needed to be, were much too dependent on high technology, and would not work well under the stress of combat.

Within a few days of the commencement of hostilities, it was clear to the average viewer that high-tech systems were working rather well. Briefings from Riyadh showed television tape of bombs landing exactly on target and doing much greater target damage than had been experienced in past wars. Dramatic strike camera pictures were exhibited early in the war which vividly demonstrated how the Iraqi air force headquarters in Baghdad was destroyed by a single precision-guided bomb. Perhaps even more dramatically, some strike camera film showed how a major structure was destroyed when a two-thousand-pound bomb was dropped through an air shaft in the top of the building. Most of the television audience was impressed and, in many cases, astounded by this precision.

Curiously, however, some newspapers, particularly in the United States, did not understand or acknowledge this performance. Critical comments continued to appear long after it had been proven to the average citizen that high technology was, in fact, working and that great precision was now a routine achievement. Many articles stated that sophistication led to complexity, complexity to unreliability, and unreliability to breakdowns. These articles argued that high-tech systems might be working in the short term, but that they probably would not work in the long term.

The best example of this lack of understanding of what was happening in the war was a report by R. W. Apple, Jr., in the

January 23 issue of the *New York Times*. One week after the war commenced and five days after the first strike camera film had been released, he asserted that greater complexity meant more problems. I criticized this article publicly on CNN because I thought it was important that the world understand that some members of the press were missing part of this story. They seemed to be blinded by the many critical articles of the past. Like Apple, they were unable, during those first couple of weeks of the Gulf War, to pick up on and acknowledge that this considerable improvement in accuracy was dramatically changing warfare and that these complex systems were performing and holding up extremely well.

I was so concerned that my favorite newspaper, the *New York Times*, was missing the story that I called Max Frankel, the executive editor. I had admired both the writing and the television commentary of Frankel for many years, ever since I was a graduate student at Columbia University in the mid-1960s. I had never met or talked to Frankel before, but he was willing to listen to me. The *Times* was missing two major aspects of the story of this war, I suggested. One was the reliability of high technology; the other was the accuracy of the military reporting coming out of Saudi Arabia. On the second point, the *Times* had published a number of articles that seemed to imply that General Schwarzkopf was "cooking" the numbers and overstating the results of the air campaign. A number of reporters and editorialists seemed to assume that Schwarzkopf and his staff were following the pattern of false reporting that developed during the Vietnam War.

I tried to explain to Frankel that the *Times* was wrong on both counts and that I was quite disturbed that the newspaper I had so admired was in the process of missing perhaps the most important story of this decade in two fundamental dimensions. He expressed interest in my concern and suggested that I write an op-ed piece for the *Times*. At about midnight that same night I dictated it to the paper.

When the hard copy of my piece was returned to me via a CNN fax machine, there were a number of suggestions for changes, some of which I found unacceptable. So I wrote Frankel, stating that I objected to these suggestions and thought it best that I forget about doing an op-ed piece. Where

I had the greatest difficulty with the *New York Times* comments on my op-ed piece was my commentary on the integrity of Norman Schwarzkopf. The point made by the *Times* editorial staff was that while it may be true that Schwarzkopf was telling the truth, he was doing it for reasons of expediency—telling the truth just to stay out of trouble.

Let me give the exact words of a *New York Times* editorial staff member in a note to his boss, Mike Levitas. "Mike. Isn't the point that, after Vietnam, they aren't going to get caught cooking the books? I don't want to gainsay Schwarzkopf's integrity, but that's not the point. The main thing is that they know after Vietnam that they have to maintain credibility, that the story will eventually get out. It's a pragmatic, not a moral, issue."

Whoever wrote this, and whoever agreed to it and sent it on to me, just didn't understand Schwarzkopf. I had known Norman Schwarzkopf for a very long time. He told the truth not because he wished to stay out of trouble, but because of his fundamental commitment to integrity. Schwarzkopf understood that the only way to operate in any large organization, and particularly when leading large organizations into combat, was to be totally honest with everyone. He was fully committed to being truthful himself, to demanding integrity of his subordinates, to sensing any breakdown in integrity (as when someone overstates the results of an attack on a key target), and to making sure the truth was told.

Early in the war it appeared to me that it was almost business as usual in the coverage at the *New York Times* and *Washington Post*. There was a great deal of attention to the diplomatic, political, and economic aspects of the war, but rather limited coverage of the military. In these two prestigious newspapers, a headline each day and a few articles dealt with the war, but the front page did not reflect that a major war of great international consequence was underway. For instance, it was quite common for only three of ten front-page articles in the *Times* to be on the war.

In June 1990, the *Times* had lost its senior military correspondent, retired Marine Lt. Gen. Bernard "Mick" Trainor. He had accepted a position as director of the national security program at the John F. Kennedy School at Harvard University.

There had been an extensive search to find a replacement for Trainor but no one had been hired. When the war broke out, the *New York Times* was apparently not ready or well manned to cover the military aspects of this story thoroughly. For instance, reporters from the *Times*, on occasion, naively quoted Pentagon officials with parochial motivations for hoping that the air campaign was not succeeding. Bob Woodward of the *Washington Post* suffered from this same proclivity. He often got the facts right, but he was way off on determining what they meant. Savvy reporters know how to identify military parochialism and discount it when they hear it.

Interservice rivalry was not a major impediment to success in the Gulf War, but it did allow some reporters to be misled about the progress of the air campaign. Another unfortunate aspect of the *Times*'s reporting was the tendency toward "group think," that is, to quote other *New York Times* reporters rather than outside experts.

Somehow the two major newspapers in Washington and New York could not grasp that the Gulf War was an important story; it took them a while to adapt and cover this story well.

The *Los Angeles Times* provided, in my judgment, the best newspaper coverage during the early stages of the war, and the excellent coverage and analysis were sustained throughout. That newspaper understood very early that there was a major war going on, and that they needed to devote an enormous amount of energy and effort to covering it. So from the beginning the *Times* ran many solid articles. Every day the front page featured substantive, well-researched, and well-written articles that covered the war comprehensively. For those who may wish to study the Gulf War and how the media covered it, I suggest starting with the *Los Angeles Times*.

USA Today also did a nice job throughout the war, with lots of expanded coverage and excellent graphic depictions of various weapons systems, tactics, and strategies. A daily column was inaugurated early in the war that provided concise commentary on a certain daily issue by knowledgeable military and regional experts. This column was quite helpful to the reader interested in following the war. The reporter who pulled this column together each day, Dennis Cauchon, called many military experts to get ideas on both the hottest issues and whom he might contact to obtain some insights and some meaningful quotes. I talked to him on occasion and was impressed with his quick mind, his lack of discernible bias, and his willingness to listen and learn. *USA Today* also had excellent graphics to help explain some of the more significant airplanes, ground vehicles, ships, and missiles as well as the tactics and strategies. Somewhat like CNN in the world of television news, *USA Today* seems to be shaping the new model as far as newspaper coverage of issues, like war, which are very complex and cannot be fully explained using just the written word and photographs.

As far as the magazines are concerned, *US News and World Report* did the best job. Its issue of February 11 wins my vote for the best single issue of a magazine written and printed in the United States during the war. Gen. Michael Dugan, the former chief of staff of the Air Force, authored the story of how the first days of the air campaign were conducted. It was well written and hit each point with precision. Just as impressive was the article written about General Schwarzkopf. There had been numerous articles written on Schwarzkopf by many journalists even before the war began, but here, at last, a single magazine article caught his breadth, depth, intellect, humor, and commitment to integrity. Finally, the editorial written by David Gergen on the last page of this issue was elegantly composed; it was a thoughtful piece that touched the heart as well as the intellect.

Time magazine also did a good job of covering the war and its aftermath, while *Newsweek* was a major disappointment. For instance, in its March 18 issue *Newsweek* highlighted the "Secret History of the War." This article was full of errors; I noted more than twenty. Let me point out three. *Newsweek* seemed to think the chief of staff of the army commands troops; that Israel negotiates with the United States while Israeli bombers are airborne and ready to strike Iraq; that using jet fighters as forward air controllers is something new.

Some specialized magazines did an excellent job of covering the war. *Aviation Week, Armor,* and the *Marine Corps Gazette* deserve special mention for their excellent coverage, while the editors of *Air Force* magazine seemed unable to move fast enough to get topical stories on the war published until long after Kuwait was liberated.

As the war progressed, all the print media improved. But with such a long buildup before the war, it was surprising that some prestigious newspapers and magazines did not do well covering the military aspects of the war from day one.

It was not in the print media, however, where the biggest controversy emerged in the coverage of the war. Although there were tens of thousands of journalists reporting on this war, the reporter who received the most attention by far was from CNN—Peter Arnett. His story deserves a separate chapter.

5

The Peter Arnett Controversy

Of all the areas of controversy relating to CNN and its coverage of the war, the Peter Arnett story is by far the most important. It was a story that developed slowly. Initially, when CNN provided coverage of the Gulf War from Baghdad, there were three reporters on the scene—Bernard Shaw, John Holliman, and Peter Arnett, as well as some support people. They were delivering straight, uncensored reports out of their hotel suite in the Rashid Hotel in downtown Baghdad. Most of the news reporters from other networks had moved to the civilian bomb shelter in the basement of the hotel. The CNN crew got very high marks around the United States and the world for remaining in a spot where they could observe the bombing and antiaircraft artillery while the attacks were taking place. They reported day and night with hardly any sleep, reporting as best they could on what they saw and heard.

For the first time in history, a television network was providing sustained, almost nonstop telephone and later live TV coverage of warfare. The TV tapes showed tracer bullets, exploding antiaircraft shells, and, in the distance, exploding bombs from allied aircraft. There was at that point very little controversy and a great deal of praise for the work being done by Arnett and the other CNN journalists.

When the Iraqi government ordered all foreign correspondents to leave the country, the CNN team prepared to depart. But Peter Arnett asked to stay and was allowed to do so. He was able to get this permission for a number of reasons. CNN was well established in Baghdad; it was considered by the Iraqi government as the international television network for the world. The other American networks and journalists (print, radio, and television) were not as well known, nor were they as well established. They certainly were not as welcome. Thus Robert Wiener, CNN producer in Baghdad, was able to convince Iraqi officials that Arnett should stay.

Initially, there was very little controversy in America about his staying. In fact, the general reaction around the United States was that Arnett was a good choice as the reporter who should stay. He had observed numerous wars and won a Pulitzer Prize for his coverage of the war in Vietnam. Those who were familiar with his background felt he understood warfare as well as any journalist can. In fact, he had seen more war than most soldiers would see in their lifetimes. He was viewed by many as being quite courageous in his willingness to stay in the middle of a city that was under attack.

The first controversy occurred when Arnett gave a heavily censored report about Coalition POWs, yet CNN did not say the report was censored. Tom Johnson quickly took steps to let viewers know that Arnett was being censored, but the damage was done. Many viewers became angry at Arnett and CNN.

A second controversy erupted when Arnett reported the bombing of a target that the Iraqis claimed was a milk factory producing formula for infants. Arnett reported what the Iraqis said, but quite cleverly pointed out that the sign for this particular milk factory was written in English. In this way he was able to show through the visual medium of television that there might be some reason to doubt what the Iraqis were saying. However, Arnett was heavily criticized by many viewers for conveying the suggestion that a supposed formula factory had been bombed deliberately by aircraft of the Coalition.

Quite quickly the thrust of telephone calls, faxes, and mail into CNN which had been so favorable turned critical. During the war CNN received about three thousand letters and faxes a day, and about half of these, after the Arnett controversy started building, were about him. Not all the mail about Arnett was negative, only about 60 percent. However, the letters that were negative tended to be *very* critical. Some viewers branded him a traitor. Others called him a spy or a lackey of the Iraqi government. Many viewers accused him of being anti-American. Two interviews in Iraq by Arnett increased the anger of many viewers. Arnett interviewed an American peace activist who was sharply critical of the United States' policy. Later Arnett interviewed Ramsey Clark, a former attorney general of the United States. Clark had just returned from Basra and stated that he saw no military targets hit but reported lots of damage, death, and destruction to civilian targets.

Criticism of Arnett came not just from angry viewers. Prominent Americans attacked him, including Senator Alan Simpson of Wyoming, who labeled him a "sympathizer," and the NBC military analyst Harry Summers, who suggested that he may have been guilty of treason. Senator Simpson's criticism was so harsh that the major news organizations in the United States rushed to the defense of CNN and Arnett. Senator Simpson later apologized publicly for his remarks.

Arnett's commentary continued to bother many viewers throughout the war and afterward. Their anger was not confined just to Arnett; Ted Turner also took lots of heat. The phrase "Baghdad Ted and Hanoi Jane" was heard throughout this land. Many Americans, who were still resentful of Jane Fonda's visit to Hanoi (and her support for the North Vietnamese government) during the Vietnam War, felt she had influenced Ted Turner, whom she was dating, into becoming a propaganda tool for Saddam Hussein. Other Americans, who thought that Arnett was quite courageous and was doing a fine job of reporting under extremely difficult circumstances, felt that many of his critics did not understand and support the constitutional right of freedom of the press and were guilty of McCarthyism. Emotions ran high on both sides of the issue, and months after the liberation of Kuwait, the "Arnett issue" was still foremost in the thoughts of many.

A bit later in the war came the bombing of the bunker on the outskirts of Baghdad. Arnett called it a civilian bomb shelter and pointed out that a large number of civilians were killed in the attack. He also stated that he could find no indication that there were any military people in the bunker, that there were any command and control facilities there, or that it was being used as anything but a shelter for civilians. This series of reports by Arnett aroused another major controversy.

The issue of the baby milk factory had not bothered me much, since I was uncertain of this factory's use and Arnett seemed to be doing his best to report what he saw. However, the coverage of the bombed-out bunker caused me great concern. In my judgment this was not a classic civilian bomb shelter. On the contrary, it appeared to have all the characteristics of a hardened command bunker. I pointed out on camera that I had been in bunkers all over the world and had worked during military exercises in bunkers for weeks at a time. What I saw on the television monitor in Atlanta appeared to be a classic command bunker, heavily fortified with reinforced concrete, camouflaged on the roof and surrounded by a perimeter fence. A standard civilian bomb shelter does not have a perimeter fence, because people have to be able to get into a bomb shelter quickly when the siren warning of an air raid goes off and to get out fast if the shelter is bombed. I felt it was my obligation as a military analyst to say this.

In fairness to Arnett, he had not spent nearly as much time in command bunkers as I had. He seemed to be making comments based on what the Iraqis were telling him and on the best knowledge that he had at the time. By this time many people were turning the TV off whenever Arnett came on and were castigating CNN for not yanking him out of Baghdad. Soon a large number of people began sending letters complimenting me for offsetting and providing balance to the Baghdad coverage. However, some people wrote to make a specific suggestion. They urged that I resign in protest to let people know that I could no longer be associated with a television network that allowed Peter Arnett to continue to broadcast Iraqi propaganda time and time again.

I told Executive Vice President Ed Turner that I was concerned that Arnett might be wrong on what this bunker was, and he immediately suggested I do a "perspective" on camera on this issue. I wrote a short script and left a copy of it on Turner's desk. Since what I planned to say was to be sharply critical of CNN, I wanted him to see what I planned to present on camera. Just before I taped this perspective, Turner came up to me with his hands before his chest, as if extracting a dagger I had just stabbed him with. When I asked if it was all right to use this perspective, he smiled and said, "Of course." This was an important moment for me. He did not suggest that I soften my criticism of CNN, even though I was criticizing CNN more than I was the other networks.

The following is what I said on camera. This perspective was repeated a number of times on CNN.

"Many members of the United States military are highly upset by the coverage of the bomb damage in Iraq that is appearing on various TV networks. They are particularly upset at CNN for running these stories time and time again throughout the twenty-four-hour day. They also feel that CNN may be sending the wrong message to millions of people in the Arab world.

"In the history of aerial bombardment bombing accuracies have never been better. In World War II bombing systems were so inaccurate that only half the bombs landed within three thousand feet. Night-time bombing and bombing through clouds contributed to these poor results. Results over North Vietnam were much better, but only half the bombs landed within four hundred feet.

"In Desert Storm smart bombs hit within five feet and unguided bombs on smart airplanes, such as the F-16 with its fine bombing system, seem to be averaging about forty feet. This accuracy, in combination with the firm public policy of reducing damage to the bare minimum of nonmilitary targets, should make this war the best as far as minimizing damage to nonmilitary targets and casualties to civilians. I appreciate the opportunity to make this point and would suggest to all viewers that the aviators of the Coalition are trying very hard to hit only military targets and to hit them with great accuracy. In the high-stress environment of combat, when aviators are being shot at by surface-to-air missiles and antiaircraft fire, there will always be some bombs that go astray. I would hope that all viewers will view the TV tape coming out of Iraq with considerable skepticism, especially when it focuses on bomb damage and civilian casualties. It may not tell the whole story. In fact, it may be telling precisely the story that Saddam Hussein wants to tell."

Throughout this entire period of time, I kept trying to figure out Peter Arnett. Was he biased in favor of the Iraqi government? Was he an antiwar advocate? Did his reporting in Vietnam carry over into this Gulf War? Was he fundamentally anti-American? Was he a prisoner of an outdated paradigm that assumed that the American military would, as a matter of course, bomb civilian targets? Did he assume that the United States government had begun a deliberate bombing campaign against civilian facilities?

The more I watched the Arnett coverage, and the more I talked to people who knew him well, the more I came to believe that he was a "feeler." In other words, Arnett is somebody who empathizes with the people around him. He was in Baghdad, which was being bombed quite regularly. He saw the deterioration of the community facilities, of water supply, electricity, heat, light, sewerage, and he was very empathic to the plight of the citizens of Iraq. As I began to sort this out in my mind, his principal motivation seemed to be as follows: One, to report what he saw, and two, to report in a sympathetic way the plight of the common people, who through no fault of their own were under bombardment, or at least in danger of being bombarded, almost every night.

It will take historians and much detailed analysis to figure out the full underlying truth of the Peter Arnett reporting. What, in fact, did take place and how close was he to the facts? How much was he influenced by the propaganda machine of the Iraqi government? How much was he playing to the residual antiwar advocates of the 1960s?

I have tried hard to give Arnett the benefit of the doubt and judge him as a reporter who didn't understand military bunkers very well and who was willing to accept some of the things that were given to him at face value when, in fact, they might have been wrong. I must give CNN credit for getting reporters into Baghdad, letting Arnett stay when the others departed, establishing a stand-alone TV uplink there, and helping him report an important story. The fact that CNN was there with a reporter on the scene, despite all the constraints on what he could say and what pictures he could take, I think was more of a plus than it was a minus. I do not believe, as many critics do, that CNN sold out to the Iraqi government in order to gain permission to stay in Baghdad when many other reporters were ordered out of the country.

On March 19, Arnett gave an extensive press conference before a large audience at the National Press Club in Washington, D.C. His comments about the bombing of the bunker reveal some of this thinking.

"I thought it was interesting, however, as the war did proceed, and as the bombing became more intense, leading into the bombing of the shelter, which I called civilian for a while, but which we just call 'shelter' now, because we don't really know what it was...And when the shelter was hit, it was as though it was a—you know, it was just another whole element of the air war. It was as though—it was taking it a degree further, that policy had shifted toward a policy of actually targeting the civilian population."

I think these remarks help explain much of tone and texture of the Arnett coverage of the bombing of Baghdad. He apparently thought that the Coalition was, in fact, deliberately targeting the civilian population. Arnett had history on his side: this had been the case in past wars. It was especially true in World War II, but was less true in Korea and in Vietnam, where the rules of engagement for aviators were much more restrictive.

There are four aspects of the Arnett supposition that continue to bother me. One, there wasn't much evidence during the war that would support his conclusion that "the policy had shifted toward a policy of targeting the civilian population." In fact, as he wandered around Baghdad, he saw many civilian areas totally untouched by bombs. Second, by the time of his press conference on March 19, three weeks after Kuwait was liberated, the evidence was overwhelming that this had been the most careful air campaign in history, as far as minimizing civilian casualties. Third, I would have thought that Arnett's role in Baghdad, especially when he was the only reporter there, was to report the facts, as best he could, and not make underlying assumptions about possible changes of Coalition policy about which he had very little knowledge and about which he might have been wrong. Fourth, if he wasn't sure that the bunker was a civilian bomb shelter, why did he call it that so many times?

Let me quote some additional comments that Arnett made at a press conference held soon after leaving Baghdad and before he returned to the United States, in late March. These comments help explain some of the difficult circumstances that he faced in dealing with officials of the Iraqi government.

"My weeks in Baghdad were spent oblivious to much of the reaction to CNN's war coverage. The information flow was necessarily one-way. It's only now that I am learning some of the depths of vindictiveness and slander that greeted my reportage, some from public figures with whom I've been acquainted for years.

"The reason I stayed in Baghdad is quite simple: Reporting is what I do for a living. I made the full commitment to journalism years ago. If you ask, are some stories worth the risk of dying for, my answer is yes, and many of my journalist friends have died believing that.

"There was no question about CNN staying in Baghdad. It became a question of who would do it. I had resigned myself to covering the Israeli side of the war, an important side of the story, though with less potential drama than the battlefield itself. I was summoned unexpectedly to Baghdad at the eleventh hour, when it became clear to CNN that the Iraqis might permit our coverage beyond a January 15 deadline. Would I help out?

"Upon my arrival in Baghdad on the eve of war I saw a repeat of what happened during the fall of Saigon at the end of the Vietnam War. Reporters were bailing out for various reasons. I watched with wonder as this rich journalistic prize fell into fewer and fewer hands. Four days after the war began, only seventeen journalists remained from the hundreds who had been covering Baghdad.

"Everybody out, the Iraqis said, except CNN. Even CNN isn't sure why they made that decision. Perhaps it is because CNN alone is seen globally. What the Iraqis told us is that they had found our coverage since August to have been 'fair.'

"Eventually, there was only me. The growing intensity of the war made the continued presence of a CNN producer and technician dangerously superfluous. Also at the Al Rashid Hotel was a Palestinian team that provided a flow of videotape sent overland to Amman, Jordan.

"My means of communication was an INMARSAT phone, a suitcase-size link with the world that I'd drag out each evening and aim at the heavens, while dialing into the International Desk at CNN headquarters in Atlanta. At my end, we crouched in the chill of the evening, 'we' being myself and at least one Iraqi censor, or 'minder' as these censors came to be called. I prepared a simple, two-minute script that the minder approved, and that I then read into the phone.

"But from the first day I established a procedure that I believe saved my credibility and made my presence in Baghdad a valuable one. That procedure was a question-and-answer routine between the CNN anchor of the hour and myself that followed each prepared script. The Iraqis were uncomfortable with it from the beginning because they could control neither the questions nor my answers.

"The only rule I followed in these Q&A sessions was that I would not discuss matters of military security.

"Why did the Iraqis allow these sessions? I told them from the beginning that I was risking my life in Baghdad, but I was not prepared to risk my credibility. I accepted the limitations of military security, I said, but I needed the freedom to better explore the phenomenon of being in a capital at war.

"But perhaps the most curious circumstances surrounding any story I did in Baghdad involved my interview with Saddam, conducted in the second week of the war. Five burly young men in suits and ties escorted me to a room on the second floor, asked me to undress completely, and began checking every pocket and seam of my clothing. My wallet, watch, pen and notebook, handkerchief and comb were put into a bag and taken away.

"Now fully dressed, I was taken into the bathroom and my hands were immersed in a disinfectant carried by one of the group. This was either an extreme form of security, or else, I mused, Saddam has a Howard Hughes-like phobia of germs. Then I was escorted back to the lobby, and told neither to talk to nor touch anyone.

"As I waited in the gloom, my CNN colleagues arrived after a three-day overland trip from Amman with a portable satellite video transmitter and tons of other gear. As they joyfully descended on me, I had to shout, 'Don't touch me!'

"I was taken to a late-model, black BMW and sat alone in the back seat as the driver crossed the July 14 Bridge and drove into the darkened city. It soon became clear he was checking to see whether he was being followed, taking elaborate maneuvers to throw off any possible pursuer, rounding traffic circles three and four times and weaving in and out of poor neighborhoods.

"After an hour of driving, we pulled up at a comfortable bungalow on a prosperous-looking street where all of the houses looked the same. An attendant came to the car and took me inside. The living room had been transformed into a makeshift presidential suite, with brocaded chairs, official seals and three Iraqi Television cameras, all brightly lighted by power from a humming generator. Saddam's closest aides were there.

"While we waited for the president, the group discussed in English recent programming they'd seen on CNN monitors in government ministries in Baghdad, laughing at pictures they'd seen of me operating the satellite telephone in the garden of the hotel.

"Only the information minister knew my name. Saddam's secretary asked me to spell it twice before introducing me to the president when he arrived. Saddam shook my disinfected hand. I think that all he knew about me was that I was the man from CNN.

"En route to the interview I resolved to be as tough in my questioning as the situation would allow. I was not intimidated by the prospect of encountering the man many called the Butcher of Baghdad. I figured he could do no worse to me than the constant bombing of Baghdad was threatening to do.

"Saddam unsettled me initially when he appeared. I had expected him to be in uniform, but he wore a mohair topcoat over a well-tailored dark blue suit, set off with a fashionable flower-print tie. He made small talk by asking, through his interpreter, why I had stayed in Baghdad. I replied it had become a force of habit because this was my seventeenth war. He expressed the hope it would be the last I would have to cover, and asked whether I had 'a long list of questions' to present to him. I answered melodramatically that I intended to ask him the questions to which the world wanted answers. He smiled, nodded his head and invited me over to the cameras.

" 'Let's go,' he said.

"I knew the Saddam interview might shed important light on the course of the developing war. It also might have an impact on the course of my journalistic career if I didn't set the right tone. As I began my first question, I locked eyes with him, and stayed unblinking throughout. I was as undeferential as possible. From the corner of my eye, I could see his aides stiffening and muttering, but the president seemed relaxed and, at the end, thanked me for the conversation, posing with me for pictures that aides sent over to the hotel a few days later.

"Because I am still on my way back to the United States, I have not seen enough of the commentary on CNN's coverage of the Gulf War to react to it. I know that I have been criticized, and that many colleagues defended CNN's decision to allow me to stay in Baghdad. For that I am grateful.

"Criticism I accept and expect. It's the labeling that angers me. For covering the Vietnam War the way we did, many of us were labeled 'enemy sympathizers,' if not communists. For being in Baghdad when I was, I was again labeled a sympathizer, if not a fascist.

"I'd go anywhere for a story if there was enough viewer interest and CNN wanted coverage. I'd go to hell itself for a story if someone important down there wanted to be interviewed. But then, the labelers would probably declare I was down there because I was an atheist."

My concerns about Arnett's coverage increased when other journalists from other networks began to provide reports. They often presented a perspective that was quite different from Arnett's. Antonia Rados, an Australian TV journalist, came out of Iraq on February 8 and reported the following on "The MacNeil-Lehrer News Hour": "We have been seeing every day civilian casualties, but sometimes we have to travel three hundred or four hundred kilometers to see them. So we were just wondering, some of my colleagues and me, why do we have to go so far if the Iraqi government says the main target is civilians.... I think what is important, you have to see Baghdad today is a town which is basically not destroyed."

In an interview, the president of CNN, Tom Johnson, told me about his difficulty in dealing with the criticism that erupted as a result of the Arnett reporting. Advertisers protested; some of them, in fact, dropped all their ads.. There was some pressure from the White House as well. Particularly intense was the criticism from John Sununu, the White House chief of staff. However, no one in the White House made an effort to call the chief executive officers of major firms to ask them to cancel ads with CNN or in any other way punish the network. Johnson was pleased that President Bush did not take action to penalize CNN for the Arnett coverage.

Johnson said that he handled the criticism and emotional reaction to the Arnett reporting by working hard to provide adequate perspective and balance to the coverage coming out of Baghdad. He mentioned my perspective in which I had pointed out the misleading nature of some of Arnett's broadcasts. He also had the producers modify the wording that appeared on the screen to make it absolutely clear to the viewers that Arnett was subject to Iraqi censorship.

Vice President Bob Furnad came up with the idea, which turned out to be quite a good one, to have the anchors in Atlanta and Washington ask specific questions of Arnett. The Iraqi censors could not hear the questions coming in from the United States, since they were only coming into Arnett's earpiece. Hence, CNN was able to get a dialogue going with

Arnett. This allowed Arnett to go beyond the censored reports he was filing. Johnson felt that this technique was quite helpful in getting more of the real story out of Baghdad. Arnett says that he came up with this idea, but after checking with a number of top-level people, it is clear to me that the idea was Furnad's. In any case, it worked reasonably well and clearly helped CNN get a more accurate story out of Baghdad.

As I pursued the issue of intense criticism, Johnson recalled that, as publisher of the *Los Angeles Times*, he had become used to lots of harsh criticism. For instance, he described his experience regarding certain articles in the *Times* about the plight of the Palestinians. These articles had caused outrage among members of the Jewish community of Los Angeles. Johnson said that there was enormous pressure to have the *Times* stop publishing critical articles about the Israeli government and how it was treating the Palestinians. Johnson had faced down these protests and economic boycotts of the *Times* on the Palestinian issue.

I should point out that the vast majority of CNN employees feel Arnett is a first-rate reporter who did his best to get out the story. Yet mine is a harsh conclusion. The best journalists fight hard to find and to report the truth. Arnett told me after the war that he listened to me often during the six weeks I worked for CNN. I wonder why, when I so strongly questioned the Iraqi position that the bunker was a civilian bomb shelter, Arnett didn't soften his words slightly and start using terms like *bunker* or *bomb shelter* (rather than *civilian bomb shelter*). I agree with many viewers who found Arnett's questions of peace activist Anthony Lawrence, former attorney general Ramsey Clark, and Saddam Hussein himself disappointingly mild. If there was anyone in Iraq who needed to face tough questioning during this war, it was probably Saddam Hussein. If Arnett had pushed harder against the boundaries of Iraqi propaganda, as Christiane Amanpour did after she arrived in Baghdad on February 18, I think he would have done a better job of reporting accurately what was happening in Baghdad and elsewhere throughout Iraq. In my judgment, it was Christiane Amanpour who saved CNN's reputation for high-minded objectivity. I give her very high marks indeed.

6

The Flow of Mail Into CNN

The mail and phone calls that came into CNN during the war provided a massive challenge to the CNN organization. CNN had grown used to handling and answering a steady flow of correspondence and had even dealt with a surge of mail during certain crises. For instance, there had been a lot of correspondence during the few days of the Panama invasion, immediately after the destruction of the Pan Am jetliner over Great Britain in 1989, and during an election night (and a day or two afterward). CNN knew how to handle this kind of short-term increase in letters, faxes, and phone calls.

However, the outbreak of the Gulf War presented CNN with a much bigger and longer lasting challenge. Approximately three thousand pieces of mail were coming in each day. Most were letters but about five hundred of the three thousand were faxes. In addition, there were about fifteen hundred phone calls per day. Zola Murdock, who is responsible for answering the mail, had to deal with this mammoth problem. CNN executives had established a policy through the years of answering all the mail that had a return address, and the network was anxious to continue with this policy despite the inundation.

There was a quick reaction to the large increase in mail by CNN, and a lot of people, including at least one vice president, volunteered to handle phone calls and answer the correspondence. But volunteers alone could not handle it. Very soon CNN made a decision to shift from volunteers to paid CNN employees, working on an overtime basis. Many were entry-level employees who wanted the extra pay and who enjoyed reading the mail and taking on the challenge of answering the phone calls. They also enjoyed the opportunity to provide feedback to the producers, reporters, staff members, and military analysts.

Once or twice a day I dropped by the communications center where the mail was being collected and phones were being answered to get a feeling for the concerns and opinions of the viewers. Some of the mail was fascinating. For instance, many viewers had ideas on how to conduct the war better or more innovatively; the better ideas I passed on to my contacts in the Pentagon.

By talking to these young people who were reading so much mail and answering so many telephone calls, I learned the issues that were particularly interesting, exciting, and maddening to the CNN audience around the world. These talented young people helped me find out how well CNN was performing, how tough the reaction was to some of the Arnett reporting, and how well I was doing in the minds of the viewers who took the trouble to write, fax, or call. I received about ten letters and faxes per day, and about every third day I got one that was either negative or very negative. The kind of mail I got and the flavor of that mail can be gleaned from a few of the letters and faxes.

As an international flight attendant for nineteen years (United Airlines) I have spent the greater portion of the war days overseas in the Pacific rim (Japan, Taiwan, Hong Kong, and Korea). CNN was the primary source of our information of events in the Gulf.

I would like to share with you this following story. On January 16, 1991, I worked a flight from San Francisco to Tokyo. Approximately 3½ hours into the flight our Captain (having been notified by Anchorage dispatch) informed our chief purser that the bombing of Baghdad had begun. We flight attendants were told and proceeded to search out military personnel to pass the word.

Adding to the emotional impact of the moment was the fact that the Captain shortly thereafter was able to pick up CNN coverage live as well as the President's speech and patch it in over the passenger-seat audio system.

Forever etched in my mind's eye is the picture of the cabin of our 747 with passengers and crew members alike frozen in seats grasping to comprehend the words emanating from their headsets. To be listening to the live broadcast of a war while passing somewhere over the Aleutian Islands was and still is indescribable.

The next letter was sent to CNN rather than to me.

I was surprised and aggravated that Maj. Gen. Perry Smith should criticize CNN's coverage of damage to Iraq.

Surprised, because it shows our country is embarrassed to have made known the unmerciful overkill of Iraq.

And aggravated because the "VIPs" of this war are trying to control everyone's thinking. It is evident that they are having to work awfully hard to keep this incongruous coalition together.

If our bombs are as accurate as Perry claims, why does it take as many as 2,000 sortie poundings every day? As one reporter asked at a briefing—why did it take 800 sorties to bomb 33 bridges?

Either we have awfully bad aim, which anyone in the military would deny, or we're out for total destruction.

In reply to letters like these, I tried to explain the difference between precision-guided bombs and free-fall bombs and the difference in accuracies between the two types. I also tried to point out the stresses on a fighter pilot when he is trying to hit a target very precisely but is being shot at by many gun and missile positions and how this antiaircraft fire can reduce his accuracy. In any case, I answered every letter, no matter how critical. To the critics I tried to make the point that I was receiving so many positive comments that I particularly welcomed the critical ones—they helped keep me on an even keel.

Arnett's half-truths ("I'm not being censored today." "My reports are 'cleared' by Iraqi censors just like in Israel." "Objective interviews with other pathological cases such as Ramsey Clark" etc. etc.) combine to form a pattern of collaboration with Iraq.

CNN is prepared to make money by contributing to the killing of Americans. Even so, your naiveté is incredible to think that CNN could ever become a credible news organization after Arnett.

ITN broadcasts are much more objective, as are the few ABC clips seen so far. I'm looking forward to NBC's going full time with news soon, and I'm talking with our local cable operator to have NBC, hopefully to replace CNN!

You should quit CNN to protest Arnett.

         *   *   *

Come on, CNN. Smith is still a flack for the Pentagon. It's nonsense that we can not call a cease-fire in the middle of a war. We deserve better than Gen. Smith.

         *   *   *

I agree with you fully that the media is showing too much of the wrong idea of Iraq civilian bomb damage. I went through France and Germany and no one complained. Even last night on "Larry King Live" Carl Bernstein was entertaining himself on how the press does not have certain options. They must think they are the fourth arm of the government. Thanks for your comments and please ask the liberals to currently cool it.

         *   *   *

Today, while watching Cable News Network (CNN), I had the opportunity to hear your perspective on the

"Rules for Battle Field Commanders." I found these rules not only very realistic and sound, but something that I could use on a daily basis in my work. (I am a detective/ supervisor with the Los Angeles Police Department in charge of the narcotic enforcement squad. Although the "enemy" is different, your rules, from making field decisions to integrity, definitely apply.)

The books on combat leadership I recommended were *The Challenge of Command* by Roger Nye and *The Killer Angels* by Michael Shaara.

This morning I watched you look directly into the camera and say to Saddam Hussein: "There will be a [Coalition Forces] ground attack in ten to fourteen days.' This from an American general officer??? An expert??? My God! Ted [Turner] and Jane [Fonda] should give you a raise.

*   *   *

I've heard enough Bullshit from Gen. Perry Smith. Can't you find someone with an iota of objectivity?

The above was the shortest letter I received. I wrote back, thanking the letter writer for his input and asked him if he could be a bit more specific in his criticism. I have not received a reply.

I am writing this to you to warn this armchair General Bud Perry Smith, who most likely has never heard a shot fired in anger and who has a chest full of medals he won in the NAAFI. He is calling the finest pilots in the world who fly at night which is more than his air force is doing, they really earn their medals. My youngest son is in the Gulf in the RAF and I served in the Army in '39–'45 and our cities were bombed, we know what war is, but your people do not, and you have not won a war on your own, so he can get himself back in his kennel. And also there are enough of us here even though we are getting old to come over and shut that blabbermouth up. I know your station will not say anything about this, I doubt you having the guts to. YOU tell that guy our boys are doing the most dangerous job with their Tornadoes, and if we can find the stupid clowns' address we would write him or phone him, and maybe pay him a visit, the punk.

Let's see your guts by telling the clown.

This letter came from Britain. (The NAAFI is similar to our military post or base exchanges.) I received a number of letters from Great Britain that were critical of me and my comments about the Royal Air Force. It seems British newspapers criticizing me precipitated some of these letters.

I salute your powerful outreach for having the quality reporting and analysis of General Perry Smith. In my opinion CNN and ABC have the best analysis of the Gulf War. CNN's General Smith stands head and shoulders above the others.

I especially appreciate Gen. Smith's explanation of the question, "Was it a military bunker or a civilian bomb shelter?" CNN is to be praised for allowing General Smith's report to be aired.

In summary, the vast majority of the letters, faxes, and phone calls were quite positive and supportive. I answered immediately all the letters up until the last week of the war, when I got bogged down. However, I found myself unable to answer some of the phone calls I received; there were not enough hours in the day to conduct my research, give my commentary, answer the letters and phone calls, and get a little sleep. As far as the letters and faxes were concerned, I came to the conclusion that the old saying that people only write to the media when they are angry is just not so.

I found my mail extremely uplifting. I have kept all the letters, and when I get a bit low, I plan to read them again in order to raise my spirits. I thank all who took the trouble to write me, even the critics, and I apologize for being slow in answering some of the letters.

The conscientious Zola Murdock prepared daily and weekly summaries for the top officials in CNN. Below is her summary of correspondence at the end of the first week. It is just one example of the frank analysis she provided both weekly and daily.

"The first 24 hours after the Gulf War began, CNN received approximately 3,000 calls. These figures are for calls logged by Public Information. There were many, many more calls that didn't get logged or went elsewhere in the company, probably thousands more.

"The immediate response to CNN coverage of the War was overwhelmingly positive! The compliments were more profuse and glowing than at any other time in the history of CNN. They seemed endless as we listened to one caller after another in the evening of January 16 and into January 17 express their awe and appreciation of CNN. The magnitude of the praise and congratulations from every corner of the globe cannot be overstated.

"Our correspondents instantly became 'The Boys in Baghdad' and concern for their safety was one of the major subjects prompting calls. Bernard Shaw, John Holliman, and Peter Arnett were the first heroes of the War in The Gulf.

"CNN viewers seem to think that we are the official place to call if they want to know something or to get something done. They expect us to contact the Pentagon, the White House, or their Congressman for them and that we should be able to tell them what to do in any crisis.

"Many of the calls are from military or ex-military personnel who have a battle plan, want to explain how the weapons work or want to suggest questions they feel should be addressed. At times, one in five callers had a 'War Plan.'

"Terrorism is a major subject of concern, especially for those who have travel plans. Also, reports that the President's guards carry gas masks caused concern. U.S. citizens want to know how much danger they are in and where to expect attacks.

"By Friday negative comments became prevalent. It is always the case, even when we are flooded with negative reaction, that most viewers begin by saying "I love CNN, but…"

"Throughout the week objections to the peace demonstrators were numerous and heated. Viewers contend that we are

overcovering this element and that we are not presenting
Bush's position adequately.

"Other aspects some viewers say are missing are: interviews with minority soldiers and their families and the people
behind the scenes such as airplane mechanics, etc.

"We are still getting some antiwar calls, but less as each day
passes. We have had numerous news-tip calls regarding
support-the-troops demonstrations or peace demonstrations.
Both types insist they support the troops.

"Viewers are extremely worried about our correspondents
when there is a missile attack and we keep our people on air.
They say we should tell them to put on masks sooner and take
cover. They urge our people to put safety over getting the story.

"Many calls objected to segments that contain speculation
about our military capability. But even more object to CNN
correspondents giving locations of missile hits, etc. Some
viewers believe that we have violated Pentagon guidelines.
They are convinced that CNN is endangering military
personnel.

"King Hussein prompted more than 100 immediate calls.
Most callers expressed appreciation regarding his appearance. But some wanted to know why, if he is neutral, is he
allowing the Iraqis to fire missiles over Jordan air space.
Leaving the 'Boys of Baghdad' out of it, he was the public
figure prompting the most favorable calls for the week.
Saddam Hussein prompted more negative calls than any other
public figure.

"When Bernard Shaw and John Holliman reached Jordan
there was negativity mixed with the admiring calls about
them. Some viewers concluded that since the Iraqis allowed
us to get coverage out when no one else could, we had entered
into some agreement with them.

"By the week's end the overwhelming majority of the calls
were negative. Viewers believe that we are giving away
sensitive military locations and other technical information to
Saddam Hussein. They say that we are endangering the
troops and that our coverage is traitorous.

"However, nothing compares with the negative response to
CNN's airing of the POWs. The moment CNN aired audio of

the pilots, the calls began. There were 500 calls in the first two hours. They have not stopped through this date. Never before have we encountered so many angry viewers!"

What was impressive about Murdock's summaries was her ability to summarize so much mail and phone calls so concisely. Most of all, I admired her candor and honesty throughout the war.

7

The Air Campaign

The air campaign in the Gulf War was of such enormous significance that military historians and others will study it for decades to try to determine what it tells us about planning, technology, tactics, doctrine, strategy, and leadership.

The air campaign was developed by a group of very bright planners in the Pentagon starting early in August 1990. A few days after the invasion of Kuwait, General Schwarzkopf had a discussion with Gen. Mike Loh, the vice chief of staff of the US Air Force, about having the air force develop an air option. The team chosen by General Loh to build the plan for the air campaign was the "Checkmate" division. (In the Pentagon a division comprises ten to forty officers, noncommissioned officers, and federal civil servants.) Checkmate had been operating out of a large vault in the basement of the Pentagon for more than ten years. It had done a lot of work in analyzing what a Soviet-NATO war would be like from an operational perspective. Col. John Warden, the chief strategist and long-range planner on the air staff in the Pentagon, took over the Checkmate division, recruited some officers from other military services and other divisions, and led this team from early August until war's end.

These officers in Checkmate not only understood air operations, but also had broad experience in combat analysis, war games, and combat simulations. Checkmate had another advantage; the officers were cleared for access to the highest levels of intelligence information as well as to the various compartmentalized programs (new weapons that we had developed to which security access was very limited).

This Checkmate team, consisting of officers from all the services (though most were air force officers), put the plan together in short order. This brain trust and the contributions it made provide one of the important stories of this war, because the Pentagon in this war was supporting rather than harassing the field commander and his staff. During the Vietnam War, Pentagon officials forced the field command to provide great quantities of data. One of the reasons that General William Westmoreland's staff was so large was the voracious appetite that Secretary of Defense Robert McNamara had for quantitative data. In the Gulf War, the story was different. The Pentagon concentrated almost all of its attention on supplying the field commander with weapons, support equipment, information, ideas, and so on.

Fortunately, these planners had a conceptual baseline: a seminal book, published in 1989 by Col. John Warden of Checkmate, *The Air Campaign—Planning for Combat*, which proved useful as an intellectual resource for all the air planners. In fact, everybody interested in understanding this war and why air power became the predominant military force during the Gulf War should read this book.

The air campaign, of course, was to have both a strategic and a tactical dimension. The first priority was to knock out key strategic targets, including electrical generating plants, oil refineries, communications nodes, command and control facilities, and command bunkers. By placing first priority on the strategic dimension of the air campaign, the air planners intended to make it impossible for Iraq to sustain a war or for the political and military leadership to conduct an effective military operation at the tactical level in the Kuwaiti theater of operations.

What was absolutely fundamental to the air campaign was for the strategic dimension to continue throughout the entire campaign. In other words, when emphasis was shifted to striking tactical targets in Kuwait and southern Iraq, a sufficient portion of the air-to-ground sorties had to continue to hit strategic targets in Iraq until such time as Kuwait was liberated. A week after Kuwait fell to the Iraqis, the air plan was completed. A team took the plan to Schwarzkopf in his headquarters at MacDill Air Force Base, Florida, and briefed him on August 10. The plan was a skeleton plan and did not have all the details worked out. But it was complete enough to give Schwarzkopf a solid understanding of what air power could do and how it could do it. Schwarzkopf then made a momentous decision, and as was his style throughout Desert Shield and Desert Storm, he made his decision quickly. He adopted the plan without significant reservation, even though it was a major departure from the current air-land battle doctrine, in which air power played a supporting role to a ground campaign. Schwarzkopf understood that if the President ordered offensive action against the Iraqis in the late summer or autumn of 1990, he would not have enough ground forces in place. He would have to rely on air power as the dominant force. He grasped another important aspect of this plan for an air campaign; that is, it would cause great damage to the Iraqi military with only a small loss of life on the Coalition side.

The next step was for Checkmate to brief Gen. Colin Powell and, when he also supported the plan, to fill in the details. General Schwarzkopf was briefed on August 17 on the more complete plan. He then told Colonel Warden to take the plan to Saudi Arabia to brief the commander in place there at the time, air force Lt. Gen. Charles Horner, the man who would be responsible for carrying out the air campaign. Horner, who was subordinate to Schwarzkopf prior to, during, and after the war, was the commander of the advance party that had flown to the Persian Gulf a few days after the Iraqi invasion of Kuwait.

As one might expect, there was grumbling by some air force officers in Saudi Arabia, since this plan had been conceived and developed in the Pentagon. But General Horner and his staff soon accepted the strategy when they realized that it was feasible, that Schwarzkopf liked the plan, and that it insured unity of command among the air forces of the four United States military services as well as among the Coalition nations, all under General Horner.

This point about unity of command should not be underestimated. One of the great problems in the Vietnam War related to the command of air assets. Throughout the war in Vietnam there was never a supreme air commander: the strategic bombers were under the command of the Strategic Air Command in Nebraska; the fighter bombers attacking North Vietnam were under of the Pacific Air Command in Hawaii; and the fighter bombers in South Vietnam were commanded by the Seventh Air Force in Saigon. This lack of unity led to conflicts and turf battles among the various air commanders throughout that long and agonizing conflict. Throughout the Gulf War, General Horner carried out the air campaign that Schwarzkopf was so enthusiastic about.

Horner also wisely allowed one of his key subordinates, air force Brig. Gen. Buster C. Glosson, to improvise within the general boundaries of the plan. Glosson, who was particularly open to innovation, was blessed with a first-rate team of air planners in Saudi Arabia. He was able to call upon the resources of the Pentagon brain trust in the Checkmate office throughout the war. Prior to and during the Gulf War, this Checkmate team was an important intellectual and planning resource for many top officials in the Pentagon, including the air force chief of staff, Gen. Merrill A. McPeek, and Defense Secretary Cheney. Cheney visited the Checkmate office in the basement of the Pentagon on three occasions during the war and was briefed by Checkmate on other occasions. In fact, it became a habit of Cheney's to be briefed by the team before key meetings with President Bush.

The air planners in Checkmate had studied air power history in depth. For instance, a significant lesson of the air war over Europe in 1944 was well understood by these planners. At the time of the Normandy invasion, many strategic sorties were diverted from the bombing campaign over Germany to support the Allied troops. This gave the Germans a respite from heavy bombing of strategic targets in Germany and permitted them to repair and partially rebuild the German industrial base. The respite was not to be repeated in the Gulf War. The air planners in the Pentagon and in Saudi Arabia emphasized and reemphasized strongly throughout the six-week war that the strategic dimension of the air campaign had to be given heavy emphasis at the start and, just as important, had to remain a significant part of the air campaign throughout.

The media, in general, didn't understand this point and asked, time and time again, questions such as, When are we going to stop bombing in and around Baghdad and concentrate the full bombing effort on Kuwait and Southern Iraq, where the bulk of the Iraqi forces are located? Or if we are trying to recapture Kuwait, why do we keep hitting Baghdad every night?

The air planners wanted to accomplish "strategic paralysis" and to maintain that paralysis until Kuwait was safely in the hands of Coalition forces. What these planners meant by strategic paralysis was simple. They wanted to ensure that Saddam Hussein could shout into his telephones and radios all he wanted without being able to talk to his field units, to resupply them or to boost the morale of his soldiers in the field.

The Coalition air campaign consisted of three essential features which insured its success. It was based on a solid understanding of the lessons of history, was coherent, and was sustained; there were no bombing pauses. The air campaign, however, was not carried out exactly as planned. Two factors led to modifications in the plan. There was a considerable diversion of air assets as a result of the Scud problem, and the weather was much worse than had been expected. In fact, based on fourteen years of climatological data, the weather in January and February 1991 was worse than in any of these previous years. These unexpected difficulties caused the air campaign to last somewhat longer than the thirty days that had been anticipated by the air planners. However, the general structure of this plan was followed. If the weather had been somewhat better and if a large number of air resources had not been diverted to chasing down, finding, and destroying Scud launchers and Scud missiles, the air campaign probably could have been shortened by a week or so. Moreover, it is normal for any campaign, whether it be a land, a sea, or an air campaign, to face unexpected difficulties that cause it to be modified somewhat from the original plan. It is clear that the military leaders chose to maintain the general coherence of the plan.

From a media point of view, the air campaign came vividly to the attention of the viewing public in two rather dramatic ways. On the first few nights of the war, all of the antiaircraft fire and the bombs falling and the explosions around the city of Baghdad brought home the fact that there was a war going on and that this war was clearly to be heavily concentrated in the air. Also, the viewer could readily see from the pyrotechnics over Baghdad that the aviators had lots of flak to contend with.

Having flown through similar kinds of antiaircraft fire over North Vietnam in 1968, I was able to explain why the losses of Coalition aircraft were so small despite this impressive display of antiaircraft artillery and surface-to-air missiles. I pointed out that if the Iraqi air defense radars were jammed or knocked out, it was very hard for antiaircraft artillery or a surface-to-air missile to hit a fast-moving aircraft. I also pointed out that the aircrews could outmaneuver the antiaircraft bullets by moving their aircraft aggressively out of the path of tracer bullets that were headed directly toward them. Let me explain.

As you look out of your cockpit at night, you observe many streams of tracers moving rapidly upward from various antiaircraft guns on the ground. If these tracers, which look like red balls, form a pretty line across the sky, you are safe. These bullets will miss you. However, if the tracers form a very tight pattern, the balls growing bigger and not appearing to move forward or backward on the aircraft canopy, you are in grave danger of being hit. By "jinking" the aircraft—that is, by maneuvering the aircraft rapidly—you can cause these incoming bullets to miss.

Those first nights of the war were indeed dramatic. With so

many people from around the world watching their TV sets, the CNN correspondents were explaining the situation by telephone. In addition, the TV tape that was driven to Amman and was sent to Atlanta by satellite showed an impressive display of deadly fireworks. Reporters were on the scene explaining what they were seeing and hearing while commentators in the United States, like me, described the perceptions and feelings actually experienced by attacking aviators. I was able to explain the types of antiaircraft artillery (23 millimeter, 37 millimeter, and 57 millimeter) used by the Iraqis since most were Soviet made and had been used by the North Vietnamese against us in the Vietnam War. I also made some calculated guesses as to what kinds of airplanes dropped what kinds of ordnance on what kinds of targets.

The second and even more dramatic event took place two days after the war started. Lt. Gen. Charles Horner narrated some film showing laser-guided bombs dropping down narrow airshafts into buildings and bunkers and doing great damage to those structures. Perhaps the most credible piece of strike camera footage of the whole war showed three airshafts in a large building and a laser-guided bomb going directly down through one of the airshafts and causing a major explosion inside the building. I was able to narrate that film and explain that by holding the laser precisely on the center of the target the pilot could guide the bomb neatly down that air shaft. The viewers suddenly became aware of this new revolution of air warfare. Combat aircraft could hit targets with impressive accuracy, and television could show to the world how this was done.

The media missed one aspect of the air campaign, which remains one of the important untold stories of the war. The only offensive action on the part of the Iraqi army took place at Kafji, a Saudi city just south of the Kuwait-Saudi border. Units of the Iraqi military had attacked across the border and captured this abandoned port city. However, this was just the initial phase of a planned major Iraqi offensive. While the battle for Kafji was under way, the Iraqi military began to move two army mechanized divisions (more than twenty thousand troops) south from Kuwait toward the Saudi border in order to commence the second and more powerful phase of the Kafji campaign.

Military intelligence alerted Schwarzkopf to this danger, and a major effort was launched to stop these Iraqi troops with a massive application of air power. The Coalition took full advantage of the air supremacy that had been gained in a single night; by morning the two divisions were routed. Continuous air strikes did the job, and a major offensive was stopped dead. If this offensive had gained momentum, and if these divisions had been able to move aggressively deep into Saudi territory, there would have been considerable ground engagements and heavy casualties.

Although I mentioned on CNN that something was going on in central Kuwait and that the air forces of the various military services and Coalition nations were attacking troops on the move, I did not understand at the time the full significance of this air action. For the first time in history a major ground offensive was stopped in its tracks by air power. Never again in the Gulf War did the Iraqis launch an offensive action.

All great military commanders accomplish both strategic and tactical surprise. With this sustained air campaign based on precision bombardment, day and night, Schwarzkopf had pulled off strategic surprise. Thirty-eight days after the first air attack he would achieve tactical surprise in the ground campaign.

The Schwarzkopf Phenomenon

One of the enduring stories of the Gulf War is the Schwarz-kopf phenomenon. If we are to understand this war, and how CNN covered it, we have to understand who Schwarzkopf is, his background, how his four years at the United States Military Academy shaped his character, and how his career evolved to the point where he was placed in command of more than five hundred thousand military personnel.

Norm Schwarzkopf and I were classmates at the United States Military Academy, and I had the opportunity to see his personality develop over four years of heavy discipline, demanding schedules, and constant testing, physical, mental, and moral.

Schwarzkopf is a man with an extraordinary breadth of experience. He grew up in a military family and traveled extensively overseas before he entered West Point in 1952. As a youngster he lived in Iran, and as a teenager he resided in Switzerland, Germany, and Italy. In those years immediately after World War II many Europeans faced devastation and deprivation. The United Nations Relief and Rehabilitation funds were running out, and the Marshall Plan had not gotten under way. Schwarzkopf had the opportunity to see the rubble in the cities of Germany and Italy—block after block of buildings destroyed by Allied bombing, by artillery, or by house-to-house fighting. He could see at first hand the havoc of warfare.

Schwarzkopf went to school in Switzerland and Germany, acquiring fluency in French and German. He then returned to the United States and spent his remaining high school years at a first-rate military preparatory school, Valley Forge Military Academy, where he excelled in many aspects of the program. From there, he entered the United States Military Academy at West Point.

The Class of 1956, which entered the academy on the morning of July 1, 1952, had a large component of students who had already completed one or more years of college study. A few had finished four-year programs and earned bachelor degrees. Others had studied for a year or two at a military preparatory school at Stewart Air Force Base near Newburgh, New York, or at a civilian preparatory school. Many of these young men were better prepared academically than Schwarz-kopf and perhaps more ready for the rigors of cadet life.

Norm Schwarzkopf and I were placed in the same platoon in the same cadet company (the First New Cadet Company) in "beast barracks" (as that two-month introduction to new cadet training was aptly named). We were treated like beasts. We spent the summer learning, in great detail, the thousands of rules of cadet life. We were awakened each morning at 5:50 AM, but, of course, most of us got up earlier to spit shine our shoes, police up our rooms, and get ready for another rigorous day. Every time we moved from one place to another, we had to move at double time, a kind of jog in which you keep the upper body in a position of rigid attention.

At the end of the summer we moved to our regular cadet companies, where we would spend the next four years. In

1952, there were twenty-four cadet companies of about one hundred cadets per company. These twenty-four companies were organized under two cadet regiments with twelve companies per regiment. Companies A-1 through M-1 constituted the first regiment, and companies A-2 through M-2 the second. Schwarzkopf was selected for A-1 Company, the cadet company for the tallest one hundred cadets in the first cadet regiment and I was selected for M-2 Company, which had the one hundred tallest cadets in the second regiment. Cadets in A-1 and M-2 were often labeled thyroid cases, since we were all six foot, two inches tall or taller. We preferred to be labeled "flankers," since these two companies were positioned on either flank of the twenty-four-hundred-man Corps of Cadets whenever we paraded.

Much has been written about Norman Schwarzkopf, particularly his combat experience in Vietnam and the impact of serving with soldiers who were being wounded and killed without much concern shown for them by more senior American officers. The lack of interest in the welfare of the ground soldier that Schwarzkopf observed with such anger and frustration during his second combat tour, in 1970, had significant impact on his thinking. It seems clear that he resolved that if he ever commanded in combat again, particularly at a senior level, this lack of concern would not be duplicated. These combat experiences were, in fact, very much a part of the maturation and development of Norman Schwarzkopf as a military commander.

There are, however, stories from an earlier time in his life that perhaps give a flavor of the experiences and the developing personality of Norman Schwarzkopf when he was a cadet at the United States Military Academy.

There are two specific recollections that I have of Schwarzkopf during beast barracks. The first occurred when one hundred cadets of the First New Cadet Company stood in a long line after supper to audition for the cadet choir. The word got out quickly among us plebes (fourth-class cadets) that performing in the choir was one of the best deals available. The choir traveled to New York, Washington, and other cities around the country. It allowed you, on occasion, to leave the academy and get away from the tight discipline of plebe year for a few days. On these trips a cadet could have a date, relax, or maybe even have a beer after a concert. So most of us wanted to do well during this audition.

The crusty old choirmaster and organist, Fritz Meyer, who had been at West Point for more than forty years, was conducting this audition. As has been the case for many years in military outfits, whenever we lined up for any reason, we stood in alphabetical order. Naturally, Schwarzkopf and I were both toward the end of the line. By the time we got to the front, the choirmaster, who was well into his seventies, was getting a bit weary auditioning a hundred new cadets, most of whom had terrible voices.

When Schwarzkopf's turn came, Dr. Meyer sounded the chord, and Norman sang out in a powerful voice, "Glor-y to God." The choirmaster was impressed. Meyer played other chords, and throughout the audition room the resonant voice of Norman Schwarzkopf boomed out "Glor-y to God" time and time again. Meyer signed up Schwarzkopf, who was destined to become, in his senior year, the cadet in charge of the Cadet Chapel Choir.

It was my misfortune to be standing too close to Schwarzkopf. When I launched into my best rendition of "Glory to God," I did not get as far as "God" before I was told, "Next!" I did not hear the old choirmaster, and I stood waiting for him to hit the next chord so I could, like Schwarzkopf, show off my vocal prowess. Meyer turned icy blue eyes on me and with voice dripping disdain, barked, "I said, 'Next.'" Schwarzkopf had beaten me hands down in singing.

But it was not just in singing that Schwarzkopf bested me and so many of our classmates. It was in that most vital of plebe skills, sweating, that Schwarzie proved king of the class. Early in July of 1952, it became clear to all the plebes of the class that the last event of the evening would not be much fun. Every night, after we had finished our postsupper training, came "shower formation," the final event before we collapsed into bed. At about 9 PM, with bathrobe on, towel neatly draped over the left arm (which was extended in a rigid horizontal position), and soap dish held in the outstretched palm of the left hand, each plebe had to stand at rigid attention (called a "brace") until such time as he sweated through his bathrobe, or, alternatively, sweat dripped off his nose. The first-class cadets would walk up and down in the shower area and tell us to stand straighter and to "pop up your chests," "stand tall," and "run your necks in." They also reminded us of all the dumb things we had done earlier in the day.

Again it was my misfortune to stand every night in proximity to Schwarzkopf. At about 215 pounds, he had an impressive ability to produce moisture from every pore. In a very short time, usually within ten minutes, H. Norman Schwarzkopf had sweated through his bathrobe. He was always one of the very first to have his two-minute shower. Next, he had his feet inspected by a first-class cadet and returned to his room where he had time to shine his shoes leisurely and go to bed early.

My fate was not so rosy. Like Schwarzkopf, I was also six foot, three and a-half, but I weighed in at an unimpressive 147 pounds. I was perhaps the skinniest cadet in the entire class and had barely made the minimum weight for my height (150 pounds) upon entry into the academy. My ability to sweat was equally unimpressive. Whereas it would take Schwarzkopf less than ten minutes to sweat through his bathrobe, I oftentimes never did. Each night, after about an hour, the first-class cadets would assemble around me, the last plebe still remaining among the hundred cadets in the First New Cadet Company. They would shout such pleasantries as "Why can't you sweat like Schwarzkopf?" and finally send me to the showers. So in both singing and sweating, Schwarzkopf beat me and many other new cadets of the Class of 1956 hands down.

Many people have asked me in recent months whether Schwarzkopf was clearly the outstanding cadet in our class. He was not. Most of us would have picked Bob Farris, who commanded the entire Corps of Cadets. Farris, an All-East football player and captain of the team, stood head and shoulders above us all in military leadership. His academic ability and athletic prowess were also outstanding. Most of all, he had that indispensable quality of the leader, charisma. However, Farris chose not to pursue a military career; he resigned his commission in 1959.

Of all the cadets of the Class of 1956 who chose to make a career of the military, my choice as the one with the greatest leadership ability, would be Donald Walter Holleder. He was an All-American football player and a varsity basketball player, and like Schwarzkopf he commanded a cadet company (M-2 Company) in his senior year. I served as executive officer to them both, and I would have given the edge to Holleder. He handled the enormous pressures of being a top athlete while leading a cadet company with maturity and grace. Holleder, like many others in the classes of the 1950s and 1960s, was killed in Vietnam. The multipurpose sports complex near the football stadium at West Point is named in Holleder's honor.

In comparison to such cadets as Douglas MacArthur (first in his class) or Robert E. Lee (second in his), Norman Schwarzkopf would fall somewhat short. But measured against the cadet records of George Patton and Dwight Eisenhower, Schwarzkopf would certainly shine. The bottom line is that it's very hard to predict the performance of generals from their performance as cadets at the United States Military Academy. This does not at all take away from Schwarzkopf and his superb leadership during the Gulf War, but it permits the thought that some of the talk about how he was destined for greatness from an early age may be a bit overblown.

Considering the fact that so many in the Class of 1956 had education and experience beyond the high school years before they entered West Point, it was quite a feat for someone like Norm who had entered so young to graduate in the top 10 percent of the class in both academic performance and military aptitude. He graduated 43 in our class of 480. Schwarzkopf also served as cadet captain in his senior year. Although there were nine cadet captains of higher rank—the corps, regimental, and battalion commanders—only about fifty cadets held the rank of cadet captain. Hence, Schwarzkopf was in the top 10 percent of his class in leadership, too. On the first of June 1956, at age twenty-one, he graduated with the four gold chevrons of a cadet captain on the sleeves of his dress uniform.

Many journalists have noted that bright officers don't usually go into the infantry. But these journalists miss an important point. Those officers who really cherish command, who seek the maximum number of opportunities to serve with troops in the field and who hope one day to be in a position of great responsibility as far as commanding the big units, have often chosen the infantry. In fact, most of the greatest American generals have come from the combat arms, especially cavalry and infantry, or from the engineers. So Schwarzkopf picked the infantry, as did many others in the Class of 1956, because he wanted to lead men and to move to positions of greater and greater responsibity through the years. He was committed to leadership; I saw it in his eyes and in his demeanor when he was in front of his cadet company thirty-six years ago. He found, early on, that commanding troops was uplifting. This was to become his life, his passion, his commitment, and his duty.

Another important aspect of the Schwarzkopf personality that has not been discussed much concerns integrity. When he entered West Point in 1952, Schwarzkopf and the other members of the class (680 entered, 480 graduated) received a great deal of instruction in the United States Military Academy's cadet honor code. There was a compelling reason for this special emphasis in 1952. In 1951, there had been a massive violation of the code, and it came to be known as the "cribbing scandal." Ninety cadets were expelled for cheating on examinations (or assisting other cadets by providing examination questions ahead of time). Many of these cadets were athletes from the football team; Bob Blaik, the son of head football coach Red Blaik, was one of them. It was the first major honor code scandal in the history of the military academy, and it received headline coverage everywhere.

During the 1951–52 academic year there followed a serious reexamination by academy officials of the letter, spirit, teaching, and administration of the cadet honor code. The Class of 1956, entering in the summer, was given special attention. For us there was heavy concentration on the meaning of honor, why integrity had become so important, and why military people had to be honest among themselves and with the public. Great weight was given to the absolute requirement of integrity in combat. Integrity in combat was a matter of life or death. If a unit commander to your left or your right radioed to you that his unit was in place and ready to provide support, you had to believe he was telling the truth; many of your men could die if the enemy infiltrated through an undefended position and hit your unit on its flank. And time and time again we were told, emphatically, that living a life of high integrity in peacetime was absolutely essential to ensuring integrity during the stress of combat.

Teaching integrity at West Point involved more than just teaching people not to lie or cheat or steal. Emphasis was also placed on not tolerating a lack of integrity among other cadets. It was the obligation of each cadet to contact a member of the Cadet Honor Committee if he observed another cadet lying, cheating, or stealing. Because of the concern about the cribbing scandal, cadets of the Class of 1956 probably received more instruction on the letter and the spirit of honor and ethics than any earlier class. We were taught to demand high integrity of ourselves as commanders and to insist on high integrity in our units and among our soldiers. Hence, a commitment to high integrity was another aspect of Schwarzkopf's personality that was well developed by the time he graduated.

In 1955, I had the opportunity to work directly for Norm Schwarzkopf. In the summer months of our first-class year (senior year), each of us was given a leadership opportunity. Some of us were to train the newly arriving plebes (freshmen) in beast barracks. Others were responsible for the discipline and training of the yearlings (third-class cadets or sophomores) at an off-post summer encampment named Camp Buckner, which was located ten miles to the west of the main campus of the academy. Schwarzkopf and I both were assigned leadership duties at Camp Buckner.

Schwarzkopf commanded one of the cadet companies; I was his executive officer. Each company had about a hundred third-class cadets as well as a few first-classmen. We slept in open-bay barracks. Since my bunk was next to Schwarzkopf's and I worked directly for him, we were together a lot during the summer months of 1955. I found working for him a pleasure. Some felt he was too gung ho, too rah-rah. But he had a "let's work hard, play hard, and get the troops out of the hot sun" attitude that I admired. (Incidentally, I never observed the hot temper that many have commented on recently.)

Upon graduation from West Point, Schwarzkopf chose the army and I the air force, so we went our separate ways. In succeeding years, I saw him no more than two or three times. Hence, although we were once pretty good friends, we were not in touch when the Gulf War started. Thus what interested me as I watched him on CNN from the anchor booth in Atlanta was how little he had changed. The personality that became so familiar to the world during and after the war was well developed by the time Schwarzkopf was twenty-one years old. Of course, he had grown and matured. Obviously, he had lost some hair (though not nearly as much as I had). Sure, he had put on some weight, but what had not changed appreciably was the structure of that personality, well formed in the crucible of the four demanding years as a cadet at the military academy.

Soon after the Gulf War started, I mentioned on CNN that I had known Schwarzkopf at West Point and had confidence in his leadership ability, his high sense of integrity, and his strong commitment to avoid the problem of false reporting that had occurred in the Vietnam War. When Schwarzkopf made a point of not getting into the "body-count business," it was clear that he would ensure that there would be no reporting of combat results that could not be verified.

Schwarzkopf had been taught that in order to maintain high integrity throughout his command, he had to set the example. A commander not only has to have integrity himself, but he has to be smart, quick, sensitive, and intuitive enough to smoke out anybody who is playing around with the data. Anybody who even thought about "cooking numbers" to make himself look good or to cover up a mistake would have to answer to Schwarzkopf.

Schwarzkopf, as I knew, was committed to telling the truth for two fundamental reasons: it was ethically wrong to lie and it just made a whole lot of sense to tell the truth. Reporting the truth in this war, so far as Schwarzkopf was concerned, was quite simple. His command would report what it knew and it would not report what it did not know. If the daily briefer reported that a certain number of tanks, aircraft, or ships had been destroyed, he had to be sure that those military vehicles had, in fact, been destroyed. The destruction of targets had to be verified through bomb damage assessment; that is, through photography (or other intelligence means) after the attack that showed that the target had, in fact, been destroyed.

Hence, throughout the Gulf War, there was a tendency by the military to underreport the results. This became clear to me early on as I kept asking questions of my former colleagues in the Pentagon about the data that were coming forth from the military briefings in Saudi Arabia. Without exception, everybody I talked to in the Pentagon kept telling me that we were doing better than we were reporting. I would ask why we were understating our results. My Pentagon contacts would say, "Well, Schwarzkopf just doesn't want to overstate his accomplishments." So when I sounded optimistic, particularly as I reacted to briefings that were given at Schwarzkopf's headquarters in Riyadh, it was because I had confidence that Schwarzkopf's briefers were reporting only what they were absolutely sure of.

Many members of the press just didn't understand this point. Most reporters were fully aware that there had been a lot of "cooking of numbers" in the Vietnam War and automatically assumed that Schwarzkopf, following a similar pattern, must be overstating the day-to-day results in this war. Time and time again, pundits and experts trundled out the observation that "truth is the first victim of war." Of course, it turned out that the truth was triumphant, thanks to Schwarzkopf and his staff. Prominent journalists such as Bob Woodward, who published such an article in the *Washington Post* on Monday morning, January 28, asserted that the Coalition was not doing as well as it was reporting. Woodward is not likely to win a Pulitzer Prize for that article. Only slowly did the media catch on to this fundamental point. My optimistic prediction in early February that the historians would call this the six-week war or the eight-week war, and not the six-month war or the one-year war, was based on my certainty that the air campaign was proceeding even better than it was being reported and that soon Iraq would be unable to hold on to Kuwait.

Perhaps the most interesting part of Schwarzkopf's relationship with the media concerned his plan for the ground campaign. He had studied military history carefully, including the great sweeping single and double envelopments of Hannibal, Napoleon, Guderian, and others, as well as the deception plans of previous commanders. He understood, for example, the deception Eisenhower had achieved by placing George Patton in command of a phantom army before Normandy. In order to surprise the enemy, Schwarzkopf had to take away Saddam Hussein's intelligence capabilities. He did this by destroying Hussein's capability to conduct air reconnaissance into Saudi Arabia and elsewhere in the theater, and he did it early in the war.

Once he denied Hussein access to reliable military intelligence, he then had to blind him to other sources of information. This is the area which led to the greatest press and media criticism of General Schwarzkopf. For a brief period of time, he had to deceive the enemy by fooling large numbers of journalists from various nations. He also enforced a news embargo on the media just as the ground campaign was initiated, since it was clear that Hussein and his top military officers were watching CNN and picking up reports from other media sources. Deception is an important and legitimate part of warfare, and it does include, when necessary, deceiving the media. To deceive the media in peacetime is unethical and wrong; for instance, what Vice Adm. John Poindexter did in the way of using disinformation when he was the national security advisor to the President is, in my judgment, dead wrong. However, to withhold information from the media in wartime in order to deceive the enemy is quite different. This activity is particularly important when the media is very "tuned in," numerous, active, and international. It becomes even more important when the media provides direct inputs to the enemy camp as it was doing through CNN, the BBC, and other sources.

As I talked on CNN about the potential ground campaign in the ten days before the ground activity started, I mentioned that Schwarzkopf was going to work hard to achieve tactical surprise. He had already achieved strategic surprise by using his extensive air campaign prior to the ground campaign. But now he had to think and plan in terms of tactical surprise. I mentioned on camera that we could count on Schwarzkopf's deceiving the enemy and the press; which, in fact, he did. By denying access to many of the combat assembly areas prior to the onset of ground combat, he was able to withhold from the press the fact that he had moved massive forces in position for the great single envelopment toward the north and east.

Also, he never discouraged the interest of the media in a Marine Corps amphibious operation, an envelopment from east to west across the beaches of eastern Kuwait, when, in fact, he had no intention of conducting massive amphibious operations. Most of the commentary in the media outlined the likelihood that there would be a double envelopment, with the marines conducting a major amphibious operation into Kuwait from the Persian Gulf and the armies of the coalition making some kind of sweeping operation in western Kuwait or eastern Iraq. Although the primary reason Schwarzkopf did not conduct an amphibious operation was to save lives from what might have become a bloody fight across the beach, the positive aspects of surprising the enemy were also a factor in his calculus. In fact, there was no amphibious operation, and his sweeping movement was directed much farther to the west than most pundits had anticipated. Schwarzkopf mastered tactical deception and conducted a brilliant, short, and decisive ground campaign. Again the American people applauded.

As the war drew to a close, there were two dramatic Schwarzkopf briefings. At the first one, he described in minute detail his operational strategy for the ground campaign. In describing his strategy, he even pointed out how helpful the press had been in enhancing his deception plan. This briefing was a stellar performance. Schwarzkopf was willing to tell most of the story (although he was circumspect about the work of the special operations forces). He credited everyone in his command with having done well, and explained how many lives had been saved by conducting an extensive air campaign before launching a massive ground assault. Schwarzkopf showed great respect for his commanders and his troops, a respect that included affection and a deep, emotional commitment to saving the lives of Coalition forces.

After the briefing he answered questions with quick, rapierlike responses. The most memorable part of the question-and-answer period came when Schwarzkopf was asked about how easy the ground campaign was. He answered with a question of his own. Had the reporter ever been in a minefield? The reporter said no. There was enormous power and poignancy in this short exchange. Schwarzkopf had experienced his most difficult time as a commander in Vietnam when he had many of his troops stuck in the middle of a minefield. In the attempt to rescue them, a number were killed and others were badly wounded. Lt. Col. Schwarzkopf had not observed this battle from a helicopter, but from close up, for he was in the minefield with his troops, and he was personally leading the rescue effort. It is doubtful to me that Schwarzkopf could have been such a master of this briefing and the follow-up question-and-answer session if he had not seen combat close up on so many occasions.

Schwarzkopf and his love for the troops was another issue that was misunderstood by much of the press in the early days of the war. In a late January briefing, when the war had been going on for just a couple of weeks, he mentioned that there had been a number of "KIAs" and quickly went on to the next subject. After that briefing, some members of the press pointed out that Schwarzkopf was very abrupt when he mentioned the soldiers of the Coalition who had been killed in action. What many didn't understand at that time was how hard it was for Schwarzkopf to talk about his lost soldiers without losing control of his emotions.

In his end-of-the-war briefing, Schwarzkopf did reveal those emotions. When he talked about people who had been killed, he teared up briefly. Even though the numbers had been low, every loss of life was a tragedy. All of a sudden the American people and the press understood that here was a commander who cared so much about the welfare and safety of his troops that it was very difficult for him to talk about casualties. This whole campaign—the planning, the deception, the massive and extended use of air power—focused on one thing, reducing to an absolute minimum the loss of lives of friendly forces. The loss of life of his troops was, to Schwarzkopf, the ultimate tragedy.

The farewell speech to his soldiers as they began to return to the United States was another highlight of the Schwarzkopf phenomenon. He spoke in terms that every corporal and private could understand. Some men of great intellect cannot talk to the common man and woman. The best leaders can.

The Schwarzkopf phenomenon captured the imagination of the world. He has been called by some the Eisenhower of our time, and there are, in fact, many similarities. Both had extensive backgrounds as planners; both worked well with people; both were excellent staff officers; both were popular commanders; both worked well with leaders of many nations. In holding together a delicate military coalition, Schwarzkopf had many opportunities to make mistakes beginning in August of 1990, but he proved sure-footed throughout. He did not stumble either during the prewar crisis or during the war itself. Also, like Eisenhower, Schwarzkopf has a wonderfully winning smile, lots of charisma, and plenty of personality.

However, the comparison between Eisenhower and Schwarzkopf should not be taken too far, because Eisenhower's challenges were immense, and he did not have the technology or the supremely well-trained troops that Schwarzkopf had. What is absolutely undeniable was Schwarzkopf's ability to keep everybody on his team and to gain the support and affection of his subordinate commanders and his troops.

Of course, Schwarzkopf would be the first to admit that he is not without faults. For instance, he has an explosive temper. If his helicopter or airplane was not ready on time, he would sometimes angrily chew out his military aide. If the final plan for the air campaign did not include a major attack against the Republican Guards in the first few hours, he could threaten to fire his air commander. His explosive outbreaks did not last long, and within a few hours he usually apologized. However, one unfortunate result of his size, powerful personality, intellect, and temper was that some staff officers in Riyadh were intimidated, both physically and intellectually by the commander-in-chief of Central Command.

As the war drew to a close, the media fully understood and generally appreciated the talents and the charisma of Schwarzkopf. It was four weeks after the war was over before

Schwarzkopf stumbled a bit with the media. In an interview with David Frost on PBS, he seemed to criticize President Bush for stopping the war a day or two early. By then he had built up such good will with the President and the American public that he was quickly forgiven.

On July 10, 1991, Schwarzkopf called me to answer three questions I had posed to him. In an interview he had mentioned that he was not pleased with some of the things military analysts had said on television. Was I included in that criticism? His reply was "Absolutely not." His problem was with a military analyst on another network who revealed military secrets and speculated too much on exact military options and on what Schwarzkopf might do next. In reply to my question on the unsung heroes, he told me he felt he personally had received much more credit than he deserved. In his judgment, the people who have not been recognized enough are those middle-level commanders who planned the war or who led their troops into combat. Finally, he felt that too much credit was being given to a number of agencies and staffs in the United States, including the Pentagon brain trust, Checkmate.

After additional checking, I find myself in modest disagreement with Schwarzkopf about the role of Checkmate. Throughout Desert Shield and Desert Storm, Checkmate, in my judgment, played a significant, albeit very low-key, role not only in supporting (with ideas, analysis, and research) General Horner's staff in Saudi Arabia, but also in helping senior officials in the Pentagon, including Secretary of Defense Cheney and General Powell, think through issues relating to the air campaign.

Schwarzkopf returned home to the kind of hero's welcome that only the Lindberghs and the Eisenhowers have received in the past. Despite the adulation he received from the American public he has managed to keep his perspective and has been generous in his praise of others. As retired Marine Corps Lt. Gen. Bernard Trainor, the military analyst for ABC, said to me after the war, "He did a hell of a job and deserves the credit."

9

The Military Briefings

Military briefings played a key role in how this war was reported. In Riyadh regular briefings were given by the British, the Americans, the joint Arab forces, and, on occasion, the French. These briefings were given in the late afternoon in Saudi Arabia but, because of the time zone difference, appeared on American television screens in the morning. In addition, there was a regular briefing in the afternoon hours in Washington by Pentagon officials.

In the first few days of the war, the briefers in Saudi Arabia and in the Pentagon were unimpressive. Some were not forthcoming with information; others were very nervous in front of the press; and some almost totally refused to answer questions. Within the first week of the war, the senior leadership in the Pentagon and in Saudi Arabia substituted other officers who gave these military briefings quite well, seemed comfortable with the press, and were attractive to most of the viewers.

CNN and C-SPAN and, on occasion, other networks covered the briefings live, and these briefing officers became well known to the world through their appearances on CNN and the other networks. In general, viewers saw the same official giving the briefing on each subsequent day. Thus we all became familiar with the calm, attractive, and articulate British briefer, Royal Air Force Group Capt. Niall Irving. Also in Riyadh viewers saw the chief U. S. military briefing officer, Marine Corps Brig. Gen. Richard Neal, an intense but straightforward man with a subtle sense of humor. We also got to know the affable Col. Ahmed Al-Robayan, who was the briefer for the joint Arab forces. The military briefer in the Pentagon was the grandfatherly gentlemen, Lt. Gen. Thomas Kelly, who had the key job of director of operations for the American Joint Chiefs of Staff.

The purpose of these briefings was to keep the large press corps, both in Saudi Arabia and in Washington, reasonably well informed on activities relating to the war. But the briefing officers also had another important mission. This was to ensure that the press did not become too well informed on certain matters, particularly intelligence, tactics, and troop movements. Viewers of television developed two quite different attitudes toward the briefings. Some felt that the military was withholding, from the press and the public, information that the people had a perfect right to know. Another group felt military leaders in Saudi Arabia and in Washington were giving out too much information, thus helping Saddam Hussein while endangering the lives of friendly forces.

One of the more intriguing inter-media issues of the war was directly related to the fact that CNN was carrying all of these briefings live. Members of the print media didn't like this heavy television coverage and urged General Schwarzkopf to turn off the TV cameras after thirty minutes of briefing and questions and answers, but to continue the questions and answers with the cameras off. Schwarzkopf agreed. CNN protested this decision, arguing that the people had the right to see, live and on camera, the entire briefing, as well as the entire question and answer period.

This was an area where the CNN executives and I quietly disagreed. I was rather pleased by Schwarzkopf's decision. The briefings had become longer and longer, and I was spending more and more of the day watching them, which interfered with my ability to conduct the research needed to find out what was going on behind the scenes. The discipline of the thirty-minute time limit caused the briefers to concentrate on the most important issues. The questions and answers tended to become shorter. The whole briefing process was thus made crisper and more to the point.

In general, the viewers seemed to enjoy the briefings. Whenever they took place, CNN viewership went way up. Many viewers regularly turned on television at ten in the morning (Eastern Standard Time) to catch the three briefings out of Saudi Arabia and at 3:30 every afternoon to watch the briefing from the Pentagon.

I felt that as a military analyst, I should listen very carefully and, when called upon to make comment, to point out what was new or particularly noteworthy. I felt I had another important role, and that was to ascertain what had not been said, what had been passed over very lightly, or—if a question had been asked and ducked—why that question might have been evaded. I have had experience with military briefings, having given thousands myself, including many when I was a combat pilot in Southeast Asia and visiting dignitaries came to my base in northern Thailand. Of course, I had also given and sat in on many military briefings during my five and a half years of duty in the Pentagon. For instance, I briefed the Armed Services committees of both houses of Congress and the Defense Subcommittee of the House Appropriations Committee on many occasions on air force plans and weapons systems.

I tried to interpret the Gulf War military briefings in a way that was helpful to the viewers, while at the same time not giving any secrets away. For instance, when the Saudi Air Force pilot shot down two Iraqi aircraft as they tried to attack Coalition ships in the Persian Gulf, I pointed out the importance of the event. The Saudi Air Force had gained credibility as a result of this action, but something quite unusual had also occurred: An Arab had shot down two other Arabs.

I would also discuss the backgrounds of the briefers themselves, since I knew so many of them (both American and British). I also explained the ranks of non-Americans, particularly the ranks of the British Royal Air Force (group captain is the equivalent of colonel, air commodore, of brigadier general, and air vice marshal, of major general).

These briefings were criticized by much of the press, particularly the briefings in Riyadh, because they did not provide as much detail or data as many reporters wanted. They were also criticized because most of the gun and strike camera film* that was shown portrayed the Coalition partners as doing extraordinarily well. The press demanded to see footage showing pilots who missed their targets. Although the military ignored these demands for a while, the British did show some film in which a bomb that had been aimed at a bridge missed and hit a market area, killing many civilians.

The quality of the questions coming from the press early in the war seemed unimpressive. Most of the Pentagon correspondents, as well as many of the reporters in Riyadh, had never served in the military nor covered a war before. In short, they didn't know enough to ask good questions. As a result, the briefers had it easy because the questions did not focus on the key issues, problems, and important things that were going on in the air. The press learned fast, however, and toward the end of the war the questions were much more to the point, relevant, and thoughtful.

Members of the media also soon learned what questions they could ask without getting into delicate areas, what questions would be rejected out of hand, and what questions were likely to elicit answers. Since each individual usually got a chance to ask only one question per briefing, reporters did not want to waste their questions. So both the press and the briefers learned throughout the process.

Over time these regular briefings from Riyadh and the Pentagon demonstrated to the viewing audience, as well as the media, that the individual who had the most information about the war was General Schwarzkopf. In comparison, the

---

*Most combat aircraft carry two types of cameras: a gun camera, which points straight ahead and takes pictures of missile and gun shots, and a strike camera, which points downward and takes pictures of a ground target before, when, and after it is hit by a bomb.

Pentagon did not have very good information, because military reports took time to flow back from Saudi Arabia. Initially many reporters and viewers felt that the Pentagon was withholding information because General Kelly kept saying, "I don't know." After a while the media began to understand that the Pentagon was not demanding that Schwarzkopf give high priority to sending information to Washington. When General Kelly said he didn't know something, correspondents began to believe him, and his reputation grew. In fact, if there were two superstars in this whole briefing process, it was British Group Capt. Niall Irving of the Royal Air Force in Saudi Arabia and Lt. Gen. Tom Kelly in the United States.

One of the most remarkable events of this six weeks of jousting between the media and military briefers occurred at the end of the war, when General Kelly said farewell to the press. He complimented them on their work and indicated that he had developed affection for the press corps at the Pentagon. He said he felt that they worked hard and told them he had also tried to do a good job. These remarks were greeted by applause that seemed genuine.

I believe this event demonstrated that there can, in fact, be a warm relationship between the media and the military if the military spokesman is as forthright throughout the entire process as was General Kelly. Kelly is a bright person who understands the First Amendment and the requirement for a robust, free press. The press, in turn, seemed willing to accept the fact that Kelly was an honest individual who was doing his best to inform them while still not giving away secrets. The relationship that developed was something to behold. It was one of the warmer, nicer stories of the Gulf War.

10

The Day I Almost Quit CNN

On the afternoon of February 7, I came very close to quitting CNN and going home. Shortly after noon of that day, Reid Collins, who was at the anchor desk in Washington, introduced a piece from Baghdad with the following words: "The relentless Allied air raids on Baghdad continue." I was already sensitive to the reportage coming out of Baghdad by Peter Arnett, and I did not like the sound of Collins's introduction. Something about the word "relentless" bothered me. I looked up the word in the dictionary and found relentless defined as "unremitting; continuous, pitiless, unfeeling, unmerciful, ruthless." I said to myself, "That is not what is going on over Baghdad." It was clear to me that the Coalition forces were hitting Baghdad or its outskirts almost every night but no bombing occurred during the daytime, although some Tomahawk cruise missiles were used on a few occasions. Hence, the bombing certainly was not continuous. In fact, in

The top CNN team in action. In the newsroom of the Atlanta CNN studio, Executive Vice President Ed Turner (on the right) explains his latest idea to (from left to right) Vice President Eason Jordan, President Tom Johnson and Vice Chairman Burt Reinhardt. These four plus Vice President Bob Furnad were the team that led CNN throughout the war. (photo courtesy of CNN)

Senior Vice President of CNN Bob Furnad was responsible for producing news twenty-four hours a day throughout the war. Described by many of his CNN colleagues as a genius, the hyperactive Furnad made decisions in a matter of seconds. (photo courtesy of CNN)

The massive newsroom at the CNN Atlanta studio. The carrousels on the left are for staff writers, producers, and news editors. The four TV monitors are high on the left so that everyone in the newsroom can keep track of what is appearing on ABC, NBC, CBS, and CNN. The news desks in the center and right cover domestic and international events respectively. During the Gulf War, this newsroom was a hubbub of activity twenty-four hours a day. (photo courtesy of CNN)

The CNN control booth in Atlanta. Called the "Pit" or "A Control" this is where the moment-to-moment decisions on what will appear on camera are made. Executive producer Charlie Caudill gestures while other producers and staff people monitor sixty TV screens. Caudill, who pulled off a number of media minicoups, was promoted soon after Kuwait was liberated. (photo courtesy of CNN)

During the Gulf War CNN had two full-time military analysts. James Blackwell, an expert on ground combat and military strategy, provided commentary more than eighty times during the six-week war. (photo courtesy of CNN)

Wolf Blitzer, the principal CNN correspondent at the Pentagon, went from obscurity to international fame in the first few days of the Gulf War. His comment on the first night about a portion of the Republican Guards being "decimated" was the only significant error he made throughout the war. (photo courtesy of CNN)

John Holliman, the country boy from south Georgia, was one of the three reporters in Baghdad when the air campaign began. The viewers loved his folksy, down-to-earth style. (photo courtesy of CNN)

The controversial Peter Arnett. The only western newsperson to remain in Baghdad for the entire Gulf War, Arnett received both great praise and much criticism. Many viewers saluted his courage while many more accused him of being an apologist for Saddam Hussein, unpatriotic or a traitor. (photo courtesy of CNN)

CNN's best-known anchor, Bernard Shaw. He was in Baghdad to interview Saddam Hussein when the Gulf War broke out. His dramatic and emotional commentary during that first night of the war caught the attention and the imagination of millions. (photo courtesy of CNN)

General H. Norman Schwarzkopf dazzled the world during the Gulf War and for many months thereafter. The high level of respect of the people for a military leader is a rarity in American history. Stormin' Norman has joined Ike (Dwight David Eisenhower) and Jimmy (Jimmy Doolittle, the leader of the one-way raid on Tokyo in 1942 and winner of the Medal of Honor) as a military leader who in the twentieth century garnered the sustained affection of the American people. (photo courtesy of Department of Defense Public Affairs)

R. E. "Ted" Turner. Ted Turner was the visionary who took CNN from a dream to the media success story of this era in eleven short years. During the Gulf War he allowed the CNN team to run their own show. He was seldom seen in the Atlanta newsroom. (photo courtesy of CNN)

The navy and Marine Corps participation in the Gulf War was very diverse. This picture shows two combat ships (the USS *John F. Kennedy* and the USS *San Jancinto*) being resupplied while underway by a replenishment ship (the USS *Detroit*). (photo courtesy of Department of Defense Public Affairs)

Cooperation among the American military services was closer than in any previous war. Here we see a Navy F-14 fighter from Fighter Squadron 32 and two Navy EA6Bs from electronic warfare squadron 32 on the USS *John F. Kennedy* being refueled by an Air Force KC-135 tanker. (photo courtesy of Department of Defense Public Affairs)

Major heroes of the Gulf War were the Patriot missile batteries of the U.S. Army. Their record of intercepting Scud missiles attacking at more than 3,000 miles per hour was impressive. However, some of the Scud warheads and missile debris inflicted damage in both Israel and Saudi Arabia. (photo courtesy of Department of Defense Public Affairs)

The remains of a Scud missile after being intercepted by a U.S. Patriot missile. Explosive Ordinance Disposal personnel had to examine the Scud debris to insure that it would do no further damage to friendly forces or civilians. This debris landed thirty-nine kilometers northwest of Riyadh, Saudi Arabia. (photo courtesy of Department of Defense Public Affairs)

the daytime most people in Baghdad were out in the streets as they went about their daily routines. Also, the bombing hardly seemed pitiless. In fact, my many queries of Pentagon officials convinced me that there was a sincere attempt by Schwarzkopf, those who planned the air campaign, and the airmen themselves to reduce civilian casualties to an absolute minimum.

It seemed to me that only military facilities were being targeted in the Baghdad area and precision-guided weapons rather than unguided bombs were being used when civilians were living or working near these military targets. Moreover, the information I received indicated that some military targets were not being hit when these targets were close to hospitals, schools, and mosques. With the "relentless Allied air raids on Baghdad continue" phrase ringing in my ears, I realized that I had a problem with CNN that went beyond the Peter Arnett coverage.

I went to see Executive Vice President Ed Turner and told him that I had a serious problem with how CNN was covering the bombing of Baghdad. CNN was making it sound as if the Coalition's bombing campaign was similar to the World War II bombing of Berlin, Dresden, and Tokyo. The big story, I pointed out, was how little civilian damage there was, not how much. Repeating to him the line: "the relentless Allied air raids on Baghdad continue," I said that the word *relentless* was an error in two ways; it was wrong in both a factual and normative sense. I told Ed Turner that this issue was really bothering me and asked him to do something about it. Turner told me that the phrase that troubled me might have been written by a CNN scriptwriter in Washington and indicated to me that he would take my criticism under advisement.

That same day I received in my mailbox, along with many other communications, an impassioned but very thoughtful letter. The writer suggested that the Arnett coverage was so biased and was presenting such a distorted view of what was really happening in Baghdad that I, as one of the two full-time military analysts, should resign from CNN in protest. The suggestion was that I go public about CNN's not balancing the story properly, being guilty of passing out Iraqi propaganda, and hurting the cause of the United Nations and the

Coalition. The writer clearly felt that CNN was misleading the American public, but more importantly that it was misleading people throughout the world. The suggestion was that if I would resign in protest, it would send out a very strong message that CNN was not being objective. The writer felt that I had established myself as someone with high standards of objectivity and that my departure from CNN in protest would thus make a powerful statement.

The combination of the Reid Collins statement, the absence of an immediate reaction to my concerns, and this letter suggesting that I resign impacted heavily on my thinking. I discussed the idea of quitting CNN with members of my family. They argued against it, feeling I could balance the Baghdad story if I stayed, but not if I left. They also pointed out that I was tired and overly sensitive. They were right. I was exhausted from three weeks of high tension and very long hours. So, on their advice, I decided to stay with CNN.

But throughout the remainder of the war I continued to get letters from various sources: "General, how can you possibly work for an organization like CNN that sends out such biased reporting, particularly from Peter Arnett?" Arnett was offending the patriotism and trying the patience of many Americans. He particularly offended those who could remember World War II when the commentators and reporters were very much in favor of Allied efforts to rid the world of fascism. The strong criticisms of Arnett continued throughout the war and letters with comments like, "for shame, General, to work with an organization that also hires people like Peter Arnett," also continued to nibble at me, concern me, and cause me to lose sleep.

The lesson from this experience now seems clear to me. If you work for a news organization, you will not be able to control the editorial policy of that organization or the commentary that comes from various reporters. If you set your standards too rigidly, you probably will not be able to stay in the organization.

I had adjusted to a large organization for thirty years. The United States Air Force did things at times that I strongly disagreed with. Yet I saw value in service to the nation and the air force. My association with CNN was much more short term; hence, it would have been much easier to walk away from that organization. But as the weeks passed, I found myself becoming more connected with, and committed to, CNN. I think that can be explained by the generally high regard I developed for President Tom Johnson, Executive Vice President Ed Turner, and the producers, anchors, reporters, and staff of CNN, especially that great group in booking. These people were trying hard to be fair and objective, to present the news as it was, without a twist, bias, or slant on it. It was easy to get caught up in this kind of commitment to professionalism, accuracy, and excellence.

With the exception of Arnett, I had few problems with any of the reporters whom I dealt with, although some were certainly better than others. I did have a continuous concern about the tendency toward what I would call "breathless journalism." The name of the game was clearly to get something on the air fast and to beat ABC and the other networks. The desire to do so continued to make me uncomfortable. On many occasions when a new piece of TV tape would arrive via satellite, I asked the producers if they could give me five minutes to look at it so I would be sure I knew what I was describing when I analyzed it on camera. Often I received answers like, "Nope, you must go on now. Do your best." "You are good at analyzing film. Go for it!" That bothered me, because I know I made some avoidable mistakes.

In fairness to CNN, the network tried very hard—between times of panic when new film or data was coming in—to provide a broader strategic viewpoint, solid analysis and a "what does this all mean?" kind of approach.

Whenever I asked to do a perspective piece, or whenever I suggested that I needed to take a few minutes on the air to present a strategic analysis, I was given the opportunity to do so. At times I was not given as much time as I thought I needed to do it thoroughly, but at least I was provided the opportunity to present analysis. As the days passed after that difficult day when I almost quit CNN, I became more comfortable working with these professionals while trying to provide analysis and insight to the viewing public.

11

Where I Got My Insights

It was clear to me early in the war that if I were going to be able to provide useful coverage of this war, I needed to tap every possible military resource, both those on active duty and those in the retired community. I also wanted to gain insights from the federal civil servants who had a solid grasp of strategy, defense policy, and Middle Eastern affairs. Happily, I had been the commandant of the National War College from 1983 to 1986, and many of my former students (both military and civil servants) were now in positions of considerable influence. Most of the military people were colonels in the army, air force, or Marine Corps, or captains in the navy. Many held responsible jobs in the Pentagon, in the war colleges, or in operational units.

In addition, I had many friends and former colleagues who had recently retired from military service. Many worked for defense think tanks or defense contractors or had their own consulting businesses. These retired officers were generally up-to-date on defense issues and weapons systems; they also had many contacts throughout the government. Finally, I telephoned a few times a friend in Britain, Air Vice Marshal Tony Mason, who had written many books on military aviation and had recently retired from the Royal Air Force. His perspectives on British and European views on the Gulf War were especially helpful.

When I hurriedly packed my bags the night the war began, one of the smartest things I did was grab my Rolodex and throw it in the car. I called a whole range of people during the first week or so to try to tap their ideas and insights. Some were very helpful, others less so. I found myself concentrating more and more on a few (about a dozen) who always seemed to have something useful to contribute. These people tended to be speed readers and speed thinkers. They often referred me to articles in the newspapers, to research papers, to books, or to TV commentary that broadened my understanding of various war-related issues. I went back to them for assistance time and time again. They seemed to be willing (and in some cases anxious) to help me. In turn, occasionally I would be able to assist them in their thinking.

I suggested to the people in CNN's booking office that some of the people who were helping me were so insightful they should appear on camera. A number of them were invited by either CNN or the MacNeil-Lehrer news team or both. (I had a friend at MacNeil-Lehrer, Jonathan Spalter, who was interested in my suggestions on important topics and knowledgeable guests. We talked to each other about every other day throughout the war).

Let me describe the individuals who were particularly helpful to me and why. For issues relating to the United States Army to ground power, to ground forces, to the West Point Class of 1956, and to issues of honor and ethics, I called on Bob Sorley. He and I had been friends for many years. He, too, was a classmate of Norman Schwarzkopf's at the United States Military Academy. Sorley had just finished writing a book on Creighton Abrams, the lead battalion commander for George Patton's Third Army during World War II. Abrams later commanded our troops in Vietnam and culminated his career as the chief of staff of the US Army. So Sorley was very much up on issues relating to armor tactics, ground combat, and the lessons of World War II and Vietnam.

Sorley related to me some interesting stories about Norm Schwarzkopf during his army career after he had left West Point and after I had lost touch with him. Sorley also was helpful to me in making contact with others. In addition, he is extraordinarily well read; he sent to me many articles that broadened my thinking.

I wanted to find someone who had done a lot of war gaming, an officer who had "fought" using both computer-based and manual combat (United States versus Iraq) simulations. Colonel Sam Gardiner, US Air Force, retired, turned out to be such an invaluable resource. Gardiner is particularly knowledgeable because he not only has played many sophisticated war games but also taught operational art at the National War College. In fact, he was involved in developing the college's academic course on that topic in the early 1980s. (Operational art is concerned with how a commander at the Eisenhower or Schwarzkopf level needs to think, to plan, and to employ military forces in combat.) After Gardiner retired from the air force, he started his own business and spent much of his time developing political-military and combat simulations.

The most successful people in the war gaming business are those who develop combat simulations for future wars that seem quite plausible to their clients in the Pentagon, in major military headquarters (such as General Schwarzkopf's Central Command, the Tactical Air Command in the US Air Force and the Training and Doctrine Command in the US Army) and the war and command and staff colleges. In April 1990, at the request of the various military services, Gardiner began running combat simulations of a war between Iraq and a coalition of forces led by the United States. He simulated this war many times and in many settings for various customers, including the Naval War College and the National War College.

When I telephoned Gardiner during the first week of the war, he persuaded me that, in a ground campaign, the first four to six hours are vitally important. If, in that phase, you can achieve your initial goals, establish some breakthroughs, achieve tactical surprise, and succeed with your deception plan, the chances are that the rest of the battle will turn in your favor quite quickly. I was able to make this point on camera on a number of occasions in the week or so before the ground campaign commenced. Of course, Gardiner proved absolutely correct on this point.

Gardiner, although a retired air force officer, was a skeptic about the prospect of air power winning the war without an accompanying ground campaign. He kept reminding me that, in the end, the ground forces would have to play an important role. Since he knew me so well from our years together at the National War College and was aware of my tendency to be optimistic, he also cautioned me about this inclination to view events in too positive a light. I called Gardiner as many as four or five times a day; he was always a willing resource. I managed to get him on camera at the CNN studio in Washington, and he did so well that he was invited back six more times.

Someone who helped me and others at CNN with our research was Bill Donnis of the book wholesaler, Byrrd Enterprises of Alexandria, Virginia. At my telephone request early in the war, he sent me (at no charge) about twenty recent books on military weapons, most of which included fine pictures, graphics, and detailed descriptions of tanks, ships, planes, missiles, guns, and other military equipment. Also, Fritz Heinzen, military book expert for Brentano's, asked publishers to send me the best new books and man-uscripts. I presented these books to the CNN graphics shop to augment their meager collection.

I had a number of sources in the Pentagon. Two were absolutely essential. Both held key positions and had direct access to senior decision makers. Although I will identify a number of Pentagon officials who assisted me, I have chosen not to identify the two who were the most helpful. Their names will not be highlighted in this book, not because they gave me any classified information, for neither of them did, but because they filled me in on the thinking and the concerns of top officials with whom they had close contact. To identify them would violate an unspoken trust and could jeopardize their careers. These two people told me that key

Pentagon officials were worried that Saddam Hussein would suck us into a ground war too early. They also were concerned during the first week or so about public reaction to the war and the possible impact of antiwar protests on the conduct of the war. This background information was extremely valuable to me and allowed me to make my analysis with more confidence. These two invaluable Pentagon officials were very discreet, but they fully understood that if I were going to provide useful analysis, I had to have not only the facts but also the context of the planning and the decision making in the Pentagon.

Many midlevel Pentagon officials were helpful to me when they served as sounding boards to my ideas. They would listen to my propositions (for example, what things the coalition might be trying or might soon try) and tell me whether I was generally on the right track. Often they would ask, "Sir, have you thought about X or Y or Z?" A mutual exchange of ideas and insights took place many times during each day.

Each day I made contact with these people between six and seven in the morning; then we carried on conversations throughout the day, sandwiched in between my commentaries for CNN. When I asked them to look into an issue, they often did research, particularly in examining relevant historical examples. Often I would telephone from the anchor desk and in a very quiet voice say, "I will be on in two minutes. Can you answer this question that just came up from the briefing in Riyadh?" Since I knew who to call on each issue, I would often get the answer I needed within the two minutes.

To a lesser degree I became an intellectual resource for the Pentagon, since I was fairly well read in military history, had written a book in 1967 on military planning during World War II, and had some ideas myself on how best to carry out the campaign. Also, I think I was helpful in sharing my ideas on what were the biggest and most interesting issues to CNN and others in the media. I made suggestions, on occasion, on ways the Pentagon could release information to help offset Iraqi propaganda. Some of that propaganda, of course, was being fed through CNN and Peter Arnett, and I suggested ways it might be offset by the release of photography, data, and gun camera or strike camera film.

An individual in the Pentagon who was a great help was Dr. Wayne Thompson, a professional military historian. He was on loan to the Pentagon from the Office of Air Force History for the duration of the war. His job was to provide the kind of wisdom that historians can share with very busy staff officers. He worked as a member of the Checkmate team that planned the air campaign and fed ideas into Schwarzkopf's staff throughout the war.

Let me explain one case in which Thompson was extremely helpful to me. When the controversy about the killing of civilians in the bunker on the outskirts of Baghdad erupted, I wanted to understand and explain to viewers the history of bomb shelters used in previous wars. Dr. Thompson did some research and explained to me what the Germans and Japanese had done during World War II to shelter themselves from the heavy aerial bombardment they were receiving. The Germans, for instance, built some superhardened bomb shelters for the elite members of the Nazi party and their families. In general, German bomb shelters were designed for easy access and egress. People had to be able to get into the shelters quickly and, if bombs hit these shelters, get out fast. In other words, ease of access was the most important feature of German bomb shelters; it was even more important than hardening. This was also true in Japan, although the Japanese bomb shelter system was nowhere near as extensive or as effective as the German system.

Dr. Thompson also gave me much data about civilian casualties in previous wars. He reminded me, for instance, that in one American raid over Tokyo in 1945, 80,000 Japanese civilians were killed. Bombing raids over German cities in 1944 and 1945 often killed more than a thousand civilians in a single 1,000 aircraft attack. He pointed out that civilian casualties due to aerial bombardment in the Gulf War of 1991 seemed to be much lighter than in any previous major war. This was due to the targeting philosophy and the availability and use of precision weapons.

Dr. Thompson and I debated when interdiction (hitting tactical targets in the enemy rear areas) had worked and had not worked in the past. We reminded ourselves of some of the lessons of desert warfare. We discussed the battle of Kasserine

Pass in North Africa in 1943, when the United States Army was beaten badly by the Germans since the Germans employed their air force, the Luftwaffe, so much better than the United States did. Since my role at CNN was to provide useful commentary, the broader my understanding of historical experiences in warfare, the better.

Maj. Gen. Jim Clapper, the director of US Air Force intelligence, was also quite helpful. Although he was extremely busy ensuring that air force intelligence resources were fully supporting the commanders in the Persian Gulf, he was always willing to talk and brainstorm with me. He and I had to be very careful in our discussions, since he was privy to so much highly classified information. But he understood my role, had a quick mind, and had great access to the kind of information I needed. He also had access to top air force leaders and seemed willing to pass on to them ideas I had gained from my perspective as a temporary journalist. I would describe to him, for instance, the hottest stories of the moment and why they seemed to interest the press. On balance he was, of course, much more helpful to me than I was to him. Incidentally, Clapper has been promoted to lieutenant general and made director of the Defense Intelligence Agency. This is generally considered the top intelligence job for a military officer within the Department of Defense.

I also received some assistance from the Army War College and, in this case, these were people I did not know. There had been a study on the Iran–Iraq War published in the summer of 1990 by the Army War College. The study was on file in the CNN library and a couple of days after the war began, a CNN staffer drew it to my attention. I called one of the authors and he gave me some very interesting background information on the Iraqi army and how it had performed in the Iran–Iraq War (poorly except in the final years). He also filled me in on the Republican Guards and on the use of chemicals and when the Iraqi military might employ them, probably only after the ground campaign started and the Iraqi army was retreating.

The commandant told me that one of the efforts the Army War College had under way involved studies, simulations, and exercises related to the post-Gulf War world. I was most encouraged to learn that postwar planning was going on even during the war, something I had viewed as extremely important. Having written a book on the postwar planning that was done during World War II, I considered it crucial for organizations in the process of conducting a war to reach out beyond the war and plan for the postwar period. Unfortunately, there was little postwar planning in the White House and the State Department during the Gulf war. If there had been and the planners had taken the "alternative futures" approach and looked at various postwar scenarios, the plight of the Kurdish people might have been anticipated and not so poorly handled.

The National War College, the school that I had formerly commanded, was also helpful on a continuing basis throughout the war. I had a situation, for instance, in which there was a requirement for expert military commentary on the battle of Kafji. This was mostly a ground battle, but James Blackwell, the CNN expert on army and marine operations, was not immediately available, so I was asked to go on camera to provide commentary. It had been a long time since I had driven tanks, jumped out of airplanes, taught infantry tactics, and fired rifles or machine guns. I needed help, and I needed it fast. I called the National War College and quickly got a marine, Col. Don Price, on the phone. I told him I was going to ask him some questions and needed brief answers. Price explained the US Marine Corps versions of the M-60 tank and the light armored vehicle. He also filled me in on the latest marine tactics, how the marines might be fighting on the offense and on the defense, and likely scenarios that might be played out.

A few minutes later, I was on camera at the anchor desk. I spoke with some authority, thanks to Colonel Price, who gave me lots of help even though we had never met. I stayed very close to the information he had just given me and was able to answer the questions from the anchor reasonably well.

Another individual who was very helpful to me was Maj. Gen. James Pfautz, US Air Force, retired, who has a strong background in military intelligence. He helped make contacts for me within the intelligence community.

In all my contacts with the Pentagon (and I had at least five hundred telephone conversations with Pentagon officials during the Gulf War), I found a very positive attitude about giving me information and insights. I think these military officers and federal civil servants felt that I was playing a useful role. The Pentagon inputs that I received gave me the confidence I needed to make my points with more certainty than I otherwise could have done. I was able to take the "Yes, I understand what's going on" approach, because I did understand fairly well what was happening strategically, operationally, and tactically during the air campaign. I was much less knowledgeable once the ground campaign commenced. Those were the days for James Blackwell to shine, and indeed he did.

In most of their contacts with the press, United States military people have learned through the years to be very careful because they have been burned so many times. In dealing with me, these military officers were talking to an individual who had lived the first fifty-one years of his life in the military, but who was working temporarily for CNN. I had been born and brought up in an army family, then served for thirty years in the air force. I was talking now to former colleagues, and in some cases friends, of many years standing. They knew me and trusted me to use the information prudently.

This leads me to suggest a point of some consequence. Within the United States military establishment there is a deep distrust of the press. This distrust is based on a perception (or an experience) that the press is trying to find areas where it can hammer the military with hard criticism. Antipress feelings in the United States military establishment may have diminished somewhat during this war as a result of the use of full-time military analysts by the television networks. For the first time since World War II, there were people working for the media whom many military officials felt they could trust completely. At times, I was almost overwhelmed by the trust these people put in me.

So what does this mean for future wars or conflicts? I believe there will probably continue to be a useful role for the military analyst who can gain information from inside sources, then provide it to the press, television, and the other media. In fact, I think it is likely that there will be even greater future use of the military analyst. For instance, I expect that the *New York Times*, the *Washington Post, Newsweek,* and other organizations that did a rather poor job of covering the military aspects of this war will conclude that they need military analysts working for them full-time: writing stories, doing research, helping to educate other reporters, and reviewing copy to screen out errors. There are a number of gifted officers who have recently retired who could serve the reading and viewing audience well in such positions. Thus I think we have seen a pattern established that will continue in the future, with retired military officers and perhaps some noncommissioned officers providing the same basic service that James Blackwell and I and some others provided in this war.

Finally, I should make a point about my own expertise. CNN picked me because I was an airman who had flown modern, high-performance airplanes, been an air force planner, and had a broad perspective on military affairs. Like CBS, CNN realized that an airman could best cover an air war. Two assets relating to high-performance aircraft that I possessed were most helpful. First, I had flown F-4s in combat in Southeast Asia and been shot at on many occasions by antiaircraft artillery of the types found in Iraq. I had also flown, in more recent years, the F-15, one of the primary aircraft stationed in Saudi Arabia. When the TV tape of head-up displays, laser-guided bombs and missiles, and other high-technology systems began to come into the CNN studio via satellite, I usually could explain to the viewers what they were looking at.

Having served as the top air force planner in those halcyon years of the early 1980s, when the Reagan administration gave us strong funding support and many of these systems were being developed, I had visited many of the defense contractors around the country and had been briefed on their programs. I was quite familiar, for instance, with the Stealth fighter, the F-117. I had spent a day at the famous Lockheed "skunk works" in Burbank, California, crawling all over some F-117s while they were in production. I asked many questions of the design engineers and production workers, thus gaining a solid understanding of a radically new type of weapons system, the radar-invisible aircraft. The next day I flew to a secret base to talk with the pilots and maintenance personnel to learn about the employment concepts and maintenance challenges of the Stealth fighter.

My years of teaching and commanding at the National War College helped me in taking a strategic perspective on issues, to include the political, economic, diplomatic, and psychological dimensions. How fortunate I was to have such breadth of assignments, operational experience, and academic education. Little did I know how much of this I would call upon in my work with CNN.

```
 ┌─────────┐
 │   1 2   │
 └─────────┘
```

Predicting the Length of the War

After the air campaign had been under way for about three weeks, it became clear to me that the war would be short and that the ground campaign would consist of rapid movements followed quickly by a major mopping-up operation. The air campaign was going very well. My contacts in the Pentagon had indicated to me by early February that the situation of the Iraqi soldiers, particularly in Kuwait, had become desperate. I decided it was time to make a prediction about how long the war would last. I wanted to do this for a number of reasons. One, I thought it would prove comforting for those viewers who had family members in the vicinity of the Persian Gulf to understand that the war would soon be over. They could then look forward to having their loved ones home within a few months.

95

I also thought there might be an outside chance that I could work on the mind of Saddam Hussein. I felt that my constant and detailed analysis of how well the air war was progressing might add to other data he was receiving and encourage him to walk out of Kuwait while his military capability was still largely intact. A few Pentagon officials encouraged me to prod him into negotiating rather than hanging on to his hard-line position. Obviously, my efforts failed.

I was somewhat reluctant to make a precise prediction on how long the war might last, fearing that I might be wrong; but, on the other hand, I didn't want to be too vague either. Early in the war there was one "expert" who said the war would last four days. Another said it would be over in eleven days. Others were much more pessimistic, predicting the conflict would last many months. A few guessed it would go on for at least a year.

Based on the information I received from the Pentagon, I decided to make a firm prediction. I made the point on CNN that the war would be referred to by historians as the six-week war or the eight-week war. This prediction was based on an examination of recent wars in the desert, like the wars that the Israelis had fought against the Arabs, which were high in intensity but short in terms of combat activity. I emphasized that there were major advantages for air power in a desert campaign, such as good visibility, the lack of tree cover, the difficulty in hiding military equipment from air attack, and the ease of finding vehicle tracks in the open desert. I also was able to extrapolate the progress of the air campaign over Kuwait into the future and make the assumption that, when more than 50 percent of the Iraqi tanks, armored personnel carriers, and artillery pieces were destroyed, a quick ground campaign would ensue and the war would be over. When the war ended at the six-week mark, many people gave me credit for a prediction that was right on the button. Most of the credit belongs to my Pentagon contacts.

Let me explain more fully the basis for my prediction. When I talked to my former colleagues in the Pentagon and told them that I was ready to predict the end of the war, I wanted them to know one of the reasons why. I felt that leaders in the United States and elsewhere needed to think hard about how long this war was going to last for planning,

13

A Television First: Full-Time Military Analysts

In the world of television journalism, something quite unusual and quite important happened during the course of the build-up to this war and the war itself. The use of military analysts on the various television networks on a full-time basis was something that had never been tried before. The networks decided before the war started that, if they were going to provide knowledgeable commentary on it, they could not rely solely on journalists and part-time military analysts. They needed to have, at the elbows of the producers, at the anchor desks, and in their research bureaus, individuals who had a thorough knowledge of military strategy, operational doctrine, tactics, and modern weapons systems. The networks also needed experts who had excellent contacts in the Pentagon so they could gain background information beyond that which could be obtained by journalists.

All the networks understood this well and undertook to find individuals who would be right for the task. What they needed were people who had extensive combat experience, had had careers in the military, had held important command and staff positions, and had recently dealt with the technology of warfare. They also wanted people who were able to present themselves before the camera in a credible way, and who were willing and able to give their analyses in fairly small packages, in other words, give short answers to questions. They also needed military experts who would be available full-time. Although not all the full-time military experts had all of the qualifications listed above, most of them did. Let's examine these people who became so familiar to the American public. I will only discuss those who appeared at least thirty times on one of the four major networks, ABC, NBC, CBS, and CNN.

Each network recruited carefully. NBC, for instance, hired Col. Harry Summers, US Army, retired. Summers is in his late fifties and a veteran of combat in Korea and Vietnam. During the latter years of his military career, he taught at the Army War College. His book on Vietnam, *On Strategy: the Vietnam War in Context*, a critical analysis of American strategy in that war, was widely read. He has continued his writing and publishes a syndicated column on military affairs. He also worked for a number of months in 1990 for CNN, but was recruited away by NBC prior to the war. Harry Summers's great strengths were his knowledge of strategy, his first-class analytical mind, his understanding of ground combat, and his ability to articulate his views both in the print media and on television.

NBC also recruited Gary Sick, a retired Navy captain who had served on the National Security Council staff, earned a Ph.D. from Columbia University, and possessed a solid knowledge of issues relating to the Middle East. But Dr. Sick was more of a strategist, Middle East regional expert, and political scientist than an expert on military affairs and military technology.

NBC also hired Lt. Gen. William Odom, a retired army officer. Odom is a West Point graduate who also has a Ph.D. from Columbia University. He had directed the National Security Agency, the major source for signals intelligence within the American intelligence community. Odom had also served for a time in the White House on the National Security Council staff. Odom's great strength, of course, was the depth of his knowledge of military intelligence. The team of Sick, Summers, and Odom covered the war pretty well for NBC. If this team of retired army and navy officers had a weakness, it was a lack of background in air warfare.

CBS had recruited a couple of military analysts with broad backgrounds. One was Gen. Mike Dugan. Before his brief stint as air force chief of staff, he had been the commander of all US Air Force units in Europe. It was a real coup for CBS to get General Dugan, with his solid knowledge of air power.

CBS also recruited Gen. George Crist, US Marine Corps, ret. Crist, a predecessor of General Schwarzkopf as commander of US Central Command, had had combat and command experience and many years in high-level staff positions in the Pentagon. He understood ground combat and had visited the Middle East and the Persian Gulf area on many occasions.

The CBS team of military analysts was well connected, balanced, and highly experienced. The only weakness of this team was the inability of either general to get much camera time. Much of their analysis ended up on the cutting-room floor. Often the CBS editors would take a taped segment of Crist and Dugan commentary of eight or ten minutes and reduce it to a minute and a half, since there were so many other segments that had to be fitted into the hour-long show.

ABC recruited Lt. Gen. Bernard Trainor, US Marine Corps, ret. Trainor had had extensive combat experience in Korea and Vietnam and had served as the top Marine Corps planner, then as the Marine Corps operations deputy (in charge of both operations and planning for the Marine Corps). After retirement, Trainor worked for a while for the *New York Times* and had a chance to cover the Iran-Iraq War. When ABC hired him, he was serving as head of the national security program at Harvard University's Kennedy School. "Mick" Trainor has a solid background in the Pentagon and a thorough knowledge of combat, especially of ground combat.

ABC also recruited Adm. William Crowe, chairman of the Joint Chiefs of Staff before Colin Powell took over that position in the summer of 1989. Crowe's overall strategic view was excellent. He had earned a Ph.D. from Princeton University, understood the Pentagon intimately, and had previously commanded American forces stationed in the Persian Gulf.

But the man ABC used most as a military analyst was Tony Cordesman. Cordesman had not had a military career, but he had written a number of books on military strategy and the Middle East. Cordesman had worked in Washington for many years and developed fine contacts on Capitol Hill, in the think tanks, and in the Pentagon. He has a sophisticated strategic view and understanding of political-military affairs.

Although ABC had assembled a very strong team, its analysts, like the NBC team, lacked anybody having a profound understanding of air combat. This might not have been much of a shortcoming in past wars, but in the Gulf War, air power was not just the dominant power; it was the only major force used in thirty-eight of the forty-two days of the war.

The networks used these military analysts for two purposes. One was to provide instant analysis of fast-breaking events. This role was especially important for James Blackwell and me. It was a somewhat less important role for the military analysts at the other networks, since these networks provided news of the war less than twelve hours a day, and therefore did not have to react quickly to as many of the fast-breaking events. At CNN, as a new TV tape came in to Atlanta, usually via satellite, or as a briefing was given, Blackwell or I would immediately react to events or comments to further analyze what had not been fully explained. We both saw our job as educators, translating complex information or confusing gun camera and strike camera film into words and concepts that would be easy for the viewer to understand. For instance, modern aircraft provide the pilot with handy symbols on the cockpit windscreen, but for those viewers who haven't flown high-performance military aircraft, their significance is hard to grasp.

The cockpit film presented on television throughout the war was generally of two types. The first showed engagements in which an aircraft from one of the Coalition nations shot down one, and sometimes two, Iraqi aircraft. Most of this film was taken from Saudi and US F-15 aircraft and exhibited the head-up display of the F-15. Having flown the single cockpit version of the F-15 for three and a half years, I understood the symbols that appeared on the windscreen in front of the pilot's eyes.

Early in the war, I asked the US Air Force to send me some colored film of a practice launch of a missile from an F-15. Using stop-action techniques, I was able to explain, in basic terms, what the pilot was seeing. Next, I would show actual combat footage and explain how the American or Saudi pilot had maneuvered his aircraft, how he had locked his radar on to the Iraqi aircraft, what the Iraqi aircraft had done to try to avoid being shot down, and how the missile had tracked the target all the way to impact.

Most of the film, however, was not of air engagements but of bombs and missiles attacking Iraqi targets on the ground. This film was also difficult to explain, but I was able to use the telestrator to highlight features on the film that were especially important. The most common footage showed laser-guided bombs. The film would display the cross hairs on the target, showing where the laser beam was pointing. The bomb had the ability to guide itself to the exact point where the laser beam was aiming. I circled these cross hairs with my telestrator pen to show where the bomb should hit.

In the next few seconds I would try to explain the military significance of the target and why the pilot may have chosen this exact aiming point. For instance, I pointed out that the best technique against bridges was to drop two separate bridge spans, one at either end of the bridge, so that repair would be very difficult. I also pointed out what to look for when the bomb impacted the target. If a hardened aircraft shelter was being hit, I alerted the viewer to look for a large explosion out of the main entrance of the shelter. If this occurred, as it often did, that meant an aircraft or munitions were inside the shelter. If there was no large explosion, then the shelter was much less likely to have housed important military equipment.

There was also some footage of electro-optical guided bombs. These were particularly interesting to watch, since a small camera rested in the nose of the bomb. The TV signal was sent back from the bomb to the attacking aircraft by a data-link system. What the viewer saw was thus quite dramatic. As the bomb came closer to impact, the view of the target got better. At impact, the camera was, of course, destroyed; but the film showed these bombs as they entered small openings in shelters and buildings.

Finally, there was some excellent footage of laser-guided missiles. The French AS-30 missile, which accelerates to supersonic speed, proved fascinating to watch. The French Jaguar aircraft has an excellent head-up display on the windscreen directly in front of (and at eye level with) the pilot. This head-up display showed the time remaining, in seconds, before impact. This time rundown helped the viewers know when to look for the missiles. Thus alerted, they could often glimpse a fast-moving missile just before it smashed into the target. Again, the telestrator was helpful in pointing out to the viewer what to look for on the head-up display, what the pilot was seeing, and the most important information to focus on during the short time (usually twenty to thirty seconds) from missile launch to impact.

Because CNN was a twenty-four-hour operation throughout the war, and because either James Blackwell or I or both were on hand for twenty hours of the day, we provided more coverage and more analysis from a military perspective than did the military analysts from the other networks. For instance, there was one day when I appeared on camera eight times. There were many days where I went on three or four times and Blackwell another two or three times. Over the forty-two days of the war, I appeared on camera well over a hundred times. Because the war was largely an air war, Blackwell appeared on camera somewhat less often than I did, but, between the two of us, we made about two hundred appearances on camera. The full-time military analysts from the other three major networks did not appear as often, nor were their on-camera segments as long as were those of the two CNN full-time military analysts.

CNN also brought many other military analysts on as guests, more than sixty people. Some, like Sam Gardiner, the war-gaming expert, appeared frequently. Through them, an enormous amount of information and analysis was provided to the viewer, who learned what the military campaign was all about, what it meant, what the implications were, and what could be expected in the future. (Appendix 3 lists the military analysts used by CNN during the war.)

The military analysts who worked at the various networks in this war played a role that was unique in the history of television journalism. What was new was that a few military analysts were available, not just part-time, but on a full-time basis to help cover a major conflict. They remained available to provide commentary on short notice throughout the day and at night. At CNN, this meant that James Blackwell and I were asked to comment within a few minutes of each new event. At the other networks, the military analysts normally had a little more time to put their thoughts together before providing commentary.

The role of the full-time military analyst is so new, and potentially so important, that it is worth examining rather thoroughly. Let me share with you some insights from one of the CBS military analysts, Gen. Michael Dugan, as well as the scheduling problems of an ABC military analyst, Gen. Bernard Trainor.

First, General Dugan. Having been the top officer in the US Air Force, albeit briefly, he was in tune with the thinking of Schwarzkopf and of Gen. Colin Powell and the other members of the Joint Chiefs of Staff. He also was fully knowledgeable about the planning of the air force for a massive air campaign in conjunction with the aircraft of the other military services and the Coalition partners. Dugan was the military analyst who was most expert on issues relating to air warfare. He knew considerably more about the concepts and technology of air warfare than I did. Since the Gulf War was largely an air campaign, Dugan was naturally better prepared to provide expert commentary than his colleagues at CBS, Gen. George Crist and Adm. William Crowe.

Dugan had a number of opportunities to serve one of the other networks, but he "waited for CBS." Dugan explained to me that he did so because he felt that CBS was the most liberal politically and the most antimilitary and, therefore, it was in the greatest need of assistance in covering the war objectively. He found CBS "monstrously disorganized." There was a great deal of competition internally between and among various news elements, such as morning news and evening news. He also observed a duplication of effort as the organization's morning and evening news subsections vigorously competed against each other rather than cooperating and sharing information and insights.

He also found that many people at CBS, particularly those in New York City, were very liberal on political issues. A number of people holding key positions, including many young women, lacked military experience, and they tended to be either antimilitary or very antimilitary. During the Gulf War, CBS seemed to be interested in asking the right questions and relied on Dugan to identify the important issues and to provide general avenues of inquiry and research. On the other hand, much of his commentary was never used. The opportunity to explicate an issue in depth was denied to him time and time again. In sum, General Dugan found working for CBS quite frustrating.

General Dugan made another interesting point. He spent much of his day, as did many of his colleagues at CBS, watching CNN. When I asked why, Dugan responded that he wanted to know what was going on and CNN was a good source. The general view at CBS seemed to be that CNN was doing a fair job of collecting the facts and providing raw television footage to its viewers. CBS saw its role during the war differently: it did not so much present the facts as interpret them for the viewer. And in this area, interpretation and analysis, the people at CBS felt that they did a much better job than did CNN.

General Trainor, a military analyst for ABC, was extremely busy throughout the war, for he provided commentary not only for ABC but also, on a regular basis, for ABC's affiliate television station in Boston WCVB. Trainor's setup was unique. Instead of spending the day at an ABC studio, he remained at his office in Cambridge, Massachusetts. Camera crews from ABC and from the local TV station were positioned there throughout the day. Hence, he did not have direct communications with the anchors (in the case of ABC, Peter Jennings and Ted Koppel). The lack of direct access to the ABC anchors was a disadvantage, particularly when it came to framing the best questions for them to ask on air.

Trainor did a great deal of *pro bono* work for public television and for various radio stations. He didn't ask for compensation, and he never received any. He continued in his job as director of the national security program at the Kennedy School.

I also did quite a bit of *pro bono* work for dozens of radio stations around the country, for the MacNeil-Lehrer News-Hour, and for Australian television and Singapore radio. I gave a few speeches in Atlanta and Augusta for high schools, Boy Scout councils, and historical societies. Most of the latter were speeches I had committed myself to prior to the outbreak of the war and felt an obligation to fulfill. Since I couldn't drive a car anywhere without falling fast asleep at the wheel, I took a taxicab or flew to each one of my speeches.

To give a flavor for the kind of military analysis that was offered during the war, I am going to quote verbatim the strategic analysis that I gave on January 23, one week into the conflict. That morning, I asked CNN vice president Bob Furnad if I might take a few minutes to do a strategic review. He asked how much time I needed and I said that I thought I could cover it in four or five minutes. Even though the war had been underway for only a short time, there had already been many articles in various newspapers praising CNN for its coverage out of Baghdad but also criticizing the network for not doing strategic analysis to help the viewer understand the war. Furnad readily agreed to my proposal to present to the viewers a strategic overview.

I thought it would be useful to review what was going on: What did it all mean and what could we expect in the future? I was being interviewed by Bob Cain, an anchor in Atlanta. I suggested that Cain make a general introduction and allow me some time to do my analysis. Here is my strategic overview:

CAIN: Good morning. We would like to look at an overview of the war's military tactics and judgment. We have with us today retired air force Major General Perry Smith. General Smith is a former commandant of the National War College. He also commanded an F-15 fighter wing in Europe. He is also the author of several books, including *Assignment Pentagon* and *Taking Charge*. The war now is just hours short of one week old.

SMITH: I think it is time to step back and take a look at our strategy and see where we are going and where we may be going in the future. I am going to recommend three books for people who might be interested in looking in more detail [at] what the war is all about.

In reflection over the course of the last forty-nine years, Americans have been involved in four major wars. I personally was at Pearl Harbor at age six and had a very exciting time in the back of a truck on the way back from Sunday school the day the Japanese bombed Pearl Harbor. So all four of those wars are clear in my mind as in the minds of people my age. War is a horrible, horrible activity, and this one is particularly horrible because it seems so unnecessary. And yet it is not the most horrible of all things, as we learned in World War II.

War is also the most complex of all human endeavors, and understanding this war is particularly difficult because of the enormous complexity of the systems. It is hard for me—and I have flown the F-15 and have been in combat many times—and it must be hard for others. So I am trying in this dialogue and in other dialogues to try to explain, as best I can, the war.

There are a number of remarkable things. We have an army general in Colin Powell who is very much like George Marshall in World War II; the overall strategist providing the overall guidance to the war. We have an army general by the name of Norman Schwarzkopf who is the Eisenhower of our time, who has pulled together and held together a very difficult Coalition with considerable skill.

What is even more remarkable is that two army generals are basically running an air campaign, because the predominant force in this war, at least during the first week, has clearly been air power. In fact, as we look forward to the future, it may well be that we have a major paradigm shift here in the sense that air power may be the prominent force and ground power in a supporting role for the very first time in major combat in the history of warfare. So that is something to think about.

The strategy itself of the air campaign is really in two phases. The first phase was the strategic phase, and that went forward in the first week and will continue into the next week. And now we are beginning to shift to the tactical phase, and that is an important phase because we are going to focus now on the forces in Kuwait and southern Iraq.

The biggest advantage that we have is clearly high technology. This is a high-tech capability against a medium-tech threat, and we are doing well in that regard. Logistics—we have a lot of advantages there. Logistics being both supplies and distribution. The distribution system in Iraq is already weak and is becoming weaker by the moment as we hit the roads and the bridges and so forth. Our supply system is really quite good.

We also have the advantage of intellect. The great advantage of democratic states is the intellectual opportunity for people to debate issues and come forward with new ideas. That is not clear in authoritarian states, and that is an advantage we have.

We have the advantage of terrain. It is hard to hide in the desert. You could hide in the jungles of Vietnam; you cannot hide in the desert in Kuwait and Iraq and that is another advantage we have.

I want to go through, if I may, just a few surprises that we have run across. One, as I mentioned, the delegation of field command. The Pentagon is not running this war. The war is being run by the field commander, as it was in World War II. That is enlightened leadership. I made some calls to the Pentagon this weekend and found some offices actually closed there, which would never have happened in the Robert McNamara period of the Vietnam War.

The second thing is low attrition. I have, frankly, been surprised that we have lost [so] few airplanes. I would have predicted that by this time, [at] the one week mark, maybe fifty or sixty airplanes. We have lost less than twenty, and that is a very happy surprise.

A third surprise is the maintenance of our aircraft. The maintenance is holding up very well. We have many units with more than 90 percent operational readiness status, which is very good after this intense first-week campaign. That bodes well for the future. We should be able to sustain a few thousand sorties a day for a very considerable period of time.

A fourth surprise from my perspective is the unwillingness of the Iraqi air force to fight. I was really surprised that they did not come up at least some time in the past few days. The disadvantage to the Iraqis, of course, is we are going after their hardened shelters, and one by one we are taking out their airplanes. So the Iraqi air force, instead of being a major problem, is going to be less of a problem in the future.

One unhappy surprise is the high losses of the Royal Air Force. Having spent eleven years in Europe and flown with the Royal Air Force, [I know] they are considered by many to be the best of the NATO air forces, and yet their losses are much higher than the losses of the other Coalition partners. I think that is partly bad luck. I think it also is partly the fact that they have been given very difficult targets to hit, but that has been one of the unhappy surprises as compared to the happy surprises.

The biggest misperception of the war, I think, was indicated in R. W. Apple's piece in the *New York Times* today. He said "greater and greater complexity means more and more glitches and more and more repairs." He is dead wrong on that. The F-15 is much easier to maintain than the F-4. [The F-4 was used extensively in the Vietnam War. In the Gulf War, a modified version of the F-4 was used to knock out radar sites with missiles.] I flew them both. I was responsible for maintaining them both. We have newer systems that are, in fact, more complex but easier to maintain. [There was more to say about reliability, but I didn't have time on the air. I give more details later in this book.]

The toughest problem is understanding Saddam himself. A quote from 1985, four years into the Iraq–Iran war: Saddam said he defined victory as "defending ourselves until the other side gives up." The biggest danger of the next week or so will be some pressures for a [bombing] pause. We must avoid that. I will stop now. There are a few other points I would like to make and I would like to recommend a few books, but I think it is time to move to something else.

CAIN: General, one quick question. You talked about the list of advantages the Allied forces in the Gulf have, and you mentioned desert terrain. Why is that any more to the Allies' advantage?

SMITH: Because we have the air power and they don't. We have the advantage of going after them. We can see the targets so readily in the desert, and they don't have air power. If they had a lot of air power, then it would be a push [that is, no advantage to either side]. I would like to recommend these books if we have time.

CAIN: Go ahead. Please list them, though, before we go any further. I think you should.

SMITH: O.K. There are three books I would really recommend. First is the fact book called *The Desert Shield Fact Book*. It is a short book. It has lots of good, hard information about what is going on over there, the units, the various types of vehicles and so forth. It is not as complete as it should be, but it is a pretty good book. The second book is a book called *If War Comes*. This is a brilliant book. It just came out about two weeks ago—by Trevor Dupuy, who has written ninety books in his long career in looking at warfare. *If War Comes, How to Defeat Saddam Hussein*. A short book, but very useful. It lays out about four or five scenarios of how the war might be fought, and I think he has done a brilliant job with this book. The third book, which we don't have a cover for, is a book called *The Air Campaign* by John Warden. He is an active-duty air force colonel who lays out the air campaign, the history of air warfare, the lessons from air warfare, and he is very much involved in the planning of this campaign.

That strategic perspective, just one of many I presented during the war, was the most thorough and required more camera time than any other. (I had told Bob Furnad I only needed four or five minutes; I actually took more than seven minutes—an eternity on a major network.)

Let me use it to demonstrate, in very specific terms, how a military analyst can get in trouble when his words are misinterpreted. When I commented that the Royal Air Force had lost some airplanes early in the war, I said that "one unhappy surprise" was "the high losses." What I said, of course, was correct. The British had lost five aircraft in the first week. But that might not seem like many until it is translated into a *loss rate.* In terms of losses per sortie during the first week of combat, it was ten times the American loss rate. There was great concern in Saudi Arabia and in Great Britain about this. At this rate, if the losses had continued, the British would, within a few weeks, have lost all the RAF Tornado aircraft in the theater.

But my comment, offered without supporting data and further explanation, was misinterpreted by the Royal Air Force in Saudi Arabia and, in turn, by some newspapers in Britain. I subsequently received phone calls from British reporters. All asked the same basic question, "Why were you so critical of the performance of the Royal Air Force?" I asked each reporter whether he had seen my comment on CNN or read the transcript. In every case, the reporter had done neither. When the calls from the press kept coming in, I went to the CNN tape library and copied down exactly what I had said. After that, each time a reporter called I would read him my exact words and ask if he thought these words were critical of RAF performance. In every case the answer was no.

Perhaps I should have been more sensitive to this particular situation and not commented on the RAF aircraft losses at all. Yet if a commentator ducks all areas that may be a bit sensitive, he will not be doing his job. In any case, I touched a raw nerve with my commentary, and the result was vilification in a number of British newspapers.

A few days later I provided a short commentary on the Saudi air force just after a Saudi pilot had shot down two Iraqi aircraft within a couple of minutes. Though I was quite complimentary about the quality of the Saudi pilots and their training and equipment, I went on to say that the Saudi royal family had a very small role to play in the Saudi Arabian air force. I was trying to counter the view that the Saudi air force was dominated by members of the royal family. The head of the Royal Saudi Air Force, I pointed out, was not "royal" (he was not one of the seven thousand members of the "official" royal family); in fact, there were very few members of the royal family in the F-15 units in Saudi Arabia.

Immediatley after I made these comments I got a call from the Saudi Arabian embassy in Washington. The chief of public relations said he appreciated my favorable comments on the professionalism and proficiency of the Saudi air force. However, he went on to point out, what I had said might be interpreted to mean that the royal family was, in fact, ducking combat and was not interested in fighting for their country. He reminded me that royal family members were flying in combat.

Once again, my facts were correct (only 5 of 150 F-15 pilots were members of the immediate royal family), but my commentary could have been misinterpreted. Happily, I was able to go on the air and straighten matters out.

These examples raise another important point. If you have a twenty-four-hour news broadcast system and you make a mistake (or if something you say is misinterpreted), you can get back on the air rather quickly and correct the error. You have a chance to set the record straight and repair most of the damage you have done. Newspapers and magazines cannot print a retraction or a clarification until the next day, week, or month. Television networks that do not run a twenty-four-hour news service can set the record straight almost immediately by breaking into regular programming, but this is not a common practice. Errors made on one of the three major network nightly news shows are normally not corrected until twenty-four hours later, if then.

In my interview with the president of CNN, Tom Johnson, we talked at length about the role of military analysts working full time during the Gulf War. He agreed with me when I suggested that there were both positive and negative aspects of having military analysts on hand at CNN throughout the entire war. Johnson said that our presence, James Blackwell's and mine, was essential to the reporting of this war, because nowhere on the CNN staff was there anybody who had the needed expertise, background, and understanding relating to military strategy and combat. He thought that our contributions were both essential and well balanced.

But Johnson said there are some dangers in this kind of arrangement. One of the dangers is that there could be military analysts who had hidden agendas or who might be manipulated by someone who was pushing a particular point of view. Johnson felt that it was therefore important to be careful about who was picked and to ensure that they were people with strong records of objectivity and integrity. He felt that it had worked out well for CNN this time, but that it was an issue that needed to be carefully monitored, particularly in the future selection of military analysts.

I asked whether military analysts could provide a bridge between the press and the military. Johnson agreed that they could and felt that this arrangement was, in fact, a very useful vehicle for getting the story out. Had he ever felt that Blackwell and I were propagandists for the Pentagon? No, he had never had that feeling.

14

The Crucial Role of the CNN Producer

Since CNN is a producer's network, what producers do and how they make decisions determines what is shown (and not shown) on Cable News Network. Let's take a close look at how a CNN producer spent his or her day and the kinds of decisions that were made during the Gulf War. I will concentrate my attention on the supervising producers, who provide overall policy guidance, and the executive producers, who are responsible for the three-hour blocks of program time. Let's assume that an executive producer's three-hour block of time was the four to seven PM period.

The executive producer would arise each morning about 7 AM and immediately turn on CNN and the other networks to catch up on what had happened during the night. Even at this early hour, the producer was already trying to identify the stories likely to become important later that afternoon. As soon as a cup of coffee was in hand, it was time to get on a personal computer at home, which was tied in through a modem to the CNN Basys system. The producer reviewed the news wires for AP, UPI, Reuters and any others that seemed to be relevant. Soon it was time to check the CNN "Read Me War" file. There were also newspapers to read. The purpose of this research was to check out the events that might linger into the afternoon hours, to pick up on new fast-breaking stories, and to anticipate upcoming events.

The drive to the CNN Studio for a ten o'clock arrival was also a time for work. The car radio was on, and the local CNN radio station was usually tuned in. Upon arrival at the station, the executive producer held a meeting with the three producers who would put on each of the three hours in the allotted time block. Together they reviewed the major stories of the day, how they would be handled, the time that would be allocated to each story from each location, and which reporters in which locations would handle each story. Also covered were the stories that required graphics and who would best provide the information to the graphics people. Surprisingly, most graphics were not constructed until an hour of two before the show; this ensured that the most up-to-date and topical graphics were created.

During the hours before the three-hour time block, the executive producer would review TV tape, give advice and assistance to scriptwriters, talk many times to the supervising producer and to Executive Vice President Ed Turner and Vice President Bob Furnad, and spend time on the telephone talking to producers and reporters around the world. There was a constant search for ideas: how could we present this story in a more interesting manner? How could we balance this story better? What kinds of questions should we ask this guest? Were there better qualified experts whom we could grab at the last minute to cover fast-breaking stories? What were the other networks covering that we might have missed?

It is the role of the executive and supervising producers to be the strategists, and for the producers to be the tacticians. For instance, there were times when each of the three hourly producers wanted to use me. It was the job of the executive producers to ensure that I wasn't used too often and that other perspectives and insights were provided to the viewer. The senior level producers knew that a large portion of the viewing audience was watching CNN for many hours every day, so they worked very hard to bring in fresh stories and to avoid repeating the same material. On the other hand, if a story was a big one, it had to be covered often to help the viewer who had just tuned in gain a balanced perspective on what was happening. Like orchestra conductors, the executive and supervising producers were in the business of making great music. In this case the music they were striving for was great television and fascinating news coverage.

Let me cite a specific example of a supervising producer at work and the ways he used innovation to make a story more dramatic, interesting, and credible to the viewer. One day early in the air campaign, I was sitting at the anchor desk watching the afternoon Pentagon briefing and waiting to comment on it. Suddenly I heard a cheer from the CNN control room. I looked to the rear and saw twenty people jumping up and down, giving each other "high fives" and patting each other on the back.

Two events, as it turned out, had come together dramatically. The Israelis had been hammered by Scuds and were at the point of retaliation when the United States decided to offer Israel American-manned Patriot missiles. These American Patriot units were fully operational and stationed in Western Europe. When Secretary of Defense Cheney told the military he wanted the Patriots sent to Israel fast, there was steel in his voice. This was a huge issue, not only for the Israelis, but for a large number of Americans and other individuals throughout the world.

CNN wanted to cover the arrival of the Patriots in Israel. Air Force C-5 airplanes were flying them from Europe into Tel Aviv. Charlie Caudill, one of the supervising producers, was in the pit in Atlanta when he received a call from a staff member: TV tape of the Patriots' arrival in Israel was about to come into Atlanta by satellite.

At the same time, the daily afternoon briefing was going on at the Pentagon. CNN did not wish to cut away from the briefing since briefings had high viewer interest. But CNN did not want to lose the Patriot story. So Caudill, talking directly to Wolf Blitzer at the Pentagon through his earpiece, told Blitzer to ask Pete Williams about the Patriots. Pete Williams, the assistant secretary of defense for public affairs, had just replied to questions and was ready to turn the briefing over to Lt. Gen. Tom Kelly. As Williams was about to leave the podium, Blitzer got his attention and asked him a question relating to the Patroits coming to Israel. At that moment the pictures began coming in over the satellite linkup.

So in one corner of the television screen viewers could see Pete Williams talking about the Patriots arriving in Tel Aviv and on the rest of the screen pictures of the Patriots arriving and being unloaded.

The story was doubly dramatic. Viewers did not have to rely solely on what Williams was saying. They could see what was happening and know that what he was saying was absolutely correct. This was good television journalism. Although it was not a part of CNN's plan to enhance the credibility of Williams, this coverage did so. It was a mini-coup for CNN; and no other network was able to do it.

Caudill, in my book, gets credit for quick and creative thinking. A less innovative producer (or a producer who did not have the authority to make quick decisions) would have cut away from the Pentagon briefing to screen the tape from Israel or waited until the briefing was over to show the Patriot arrival footage.

Such creative activities took place at CNN day after day, week after week. The empowerment of producers and the encouragement of on-the-spot innovation were two of the reasons why CNN held the attention of the viewing audience.

15

Booking Forty Guests a Day

To understand the success of CNN in the Gulf War of 1991, one has to take a close look at the role played by the vice president for network bookings, Gail Evans. She had the major responsibility of ensuring that the story of the war was presented to the American people and to the world in an interesting and balanced way. A dozen staff members under Evans in Atlanta and in Washington had the responsibility of finding between forty and fifty guests every day who would come to one of the CNN studios scattered around the world. Finding the very best people to give expert commentary and provide analysis on the Gulf War in its many dimensions—military, political, economic, cultural, historical, environmental, and psychological—was a constant challenge to the staff.

Evans has on her active Rolodex some forty thousand names. In fact, CNN in the last eleven years has booked and used more than seventy thousand guests. Evans told me that she has in her head the names of about ten thousand individuals whom she knows. During the war I threw at her at least a hundred names. She not only knew most of them, but would always give me her very candid evaluation, such as, Yes, Perry, but that person is a bit of a kook; or, That person carries some baggage; or, That person is a self-promoter; or, I forgot about him, he would be great.

If Ed Turner is the chief "news junkie" on CNN, Gail Evans is the "guest junkie." She has a finely tuned sense for people and understands intuitively their strengths and weaknesses. She also knows who might do less well, carry a hidden agenda, or have heavy biases and prejudices. Like a great football coach who can tell from a ten-minute workout whether a prospect has the skill to excel on the gridiron, Evans can sniff out talent and substance in a telephone conversation lasting only a few minutes.

Evans plays another vital role in a quiet way. She is Ed Turner's sounding board. Whenever he is troubled about an important decision or needs advice from someone with superb intuition, he wanders a few steps down the hall and has a chat with Evans.

She has assembled a team of extraordinary people, most of them women. What these bookers do is reach out by telephone to the best experts available and persuade them to appear on CNN. The bookers thoroughly research each guest. Most of this research is by telephone with people who are trustworthy, have good judgment, and know who is particularly strong in their areas of expertise. Each day the bookers send a list of upcoming guests to the CNN library, and every night a computer search is done on the guests through two data bases, Nexis and Dialog, which highlight recent articles written on these people in both large and small publications. There have been a number of occasions when this careful research revealed that an upcoming guest was, in one way or another, inappropriate.

CNN's reputation as a responsible news organization is constantly on the minds of the bookers. They want articulate people who will speak to issues from various points of view. However, they live in fear that they will put someone on camera and list his or her credentials only to find out later that these credentials are phony. Screening out the impostors is a vital part of the bookers' routine. For instance, CNN had once invited a lawyer whom other networks were using extensively. The Dialog data base showed that he had been disbarred. A CNN booker called him up the next morning and told him that the interview was canceled.

Bookers lead a busy life. They constantly survey the top newspapers and magazines to determine who is writing the best op-ed pieces, who has recently published articles or books, and who has been in the news or on camera extensively. Bookers will contact the prospective guest and do a preinterview. If the prospective guest does not seem able to answer questions with short, articulate responses, the guest is gently let off the hook and never invited.

If the preinterview goes well, the guest is invited on the spot, and the details of the appearance are worked out over the phone. The bookers make sure each guest is met at the CNN security desk and made ready for appearance on camera. The bookers also make sure that, after the interview, each guest is thanked, provided transportation, and given the feeling that the contribution was appreciated. Hospitality is a hallmark at CNN, and providing it is a considerable part of a booker's job.

One of the most delicate tasks for a booker is calling a guest and canceling an appearance. It is even harder to cancel someone at the very last minute after the guest has taken the trouble to come all the way to one of the CNN studios. Fast-breaking, unexpected events are the primary reason for these cancellations. Happily, this happens less than five percent of the time. The canceled guest often expects to go on a bit later in the day, but that seldom happens, since the rest of the day is usually fully booked with other stories and guests. Most of these guests receive absolutely no compensation for their contributions, although CNN sometimes pays their transportation expenses.

My selection by Evans as a full-time military analyst during the war had an interesting twist. From August 1990 to early January 1991, Evans felt war would be avoided. After the meeting in Geneva on January 9, at which Secretary of State Baker made no progress in negotiating with Iraqi Foreign Minister Tariq Aziz on a peaceful end to the crisis in Kuwait, she saw that war was quite likely. She was fairly certain that when it did ensue, it was, at least initially, going to be an air war. She was in a panic. She needed to find an expert in air combat, and she wasn't sure who to pick. She had looked very closely, before this, at a retired admiral who had flown off carriers and had lots of combat experience. He was very attractive and knowledgeable, had only recently retired, and was excellent on camera.

However, Evans felt a nagging concern. The air campaign would be fought primarily by air force people, Evans thought, so it would be better to get a retired air force officer rather than an airman from one of the other services. Gen. Michael Dugan's name came immediately to mind. Dugan would have been a great choice for a number of reasons. He was attractive and articulate. From the point of view of publicity and pizzazz, having Mike Dugan as a full-time CNN military analyst would have been a coup, rather like the signing of a top draft choice by a major league sports team.

But the highly intuitive Evans had a lingering concern about General Dugan, too. From a journalistic point of view, Dugan might not be such a great choice. He carried some "baggage" with him. He had been fired as air force chief of staff, and many people might wonder whether the firing would color his judgment about Secretary of Defense Cheney and General Powell, who had fully supported Cheney in the decision to remove Dugan. And Evans was mildly concerned about the issue of Dugan's delayed retirement (beyond the normal ninety days) so he could retire in 1991 and receive an increased pension.

Hence, Gail Evans brought me aboard through a decision-making process that included both a process of elimination and intuition. This is the same basic process followed by each of her bookers dozens of times a day.

16

The Power of the Media

There are a number of dramatic lessons that have emerged from this war. One clearly is the extraordinary power of television at a time when people are paying great attention to world events.

Over the six weeks of the war more people watched more hours of television per day than at any time in history. Many people watched television as much as fifteen or sixteen hours a day. They just couldn't turn it off. Using remote-control devices to control the sets in their bedrooms, they would go to bed with the war and wake up with the war. If they awakened in the middle of the night, they flipped on their TV sets to see whether any dramatic new event had taken place. If they were retired, not employed outside the home, or on vacation, they would watch television throughout the day and well into the night. Family members of military people in the Gulf—an audience of more than three million—kept a constant vigil.

And they were joined by a much larger audience that also had an intense interest—veterans who had fought in other wars.

In addition to informing a large viewing audience, the various networks had an opportunity to educate senior governmental officials who were embroiled in this war. For instance, I found myself coming up with ideas and insights that I wanted to share, not only with the general public, but also with government officials. Having spent over thirty years working for the government of the United States, I had a pretty good idea of the kind of initiatives that lower-level officials might be presenting to their bosses which would get bogged down in the bureaucracy and not reach top Defense Department officials in a timely manner.

In my conversations with Pentagon officials from the rank of major through two-star general, it was interesting how often they would say, in effect, "We are trying to get something done here, but we are stuck. It would be great if you could raise the issue on CNN. That might help us get some important things done more quickly."

Let me give a specific example. There was concern in the Pentagon that the United States was not offsetting the propaganda that was coming out of Baghdad relating to damage to areas where civilians worked and lived. The Pentagon, the White House, and the CIA had photographs from satellites and reconnaissance aircraft that showed how little damage involved civilian property in the Baghdad area. Yet the US government was not releasing this film. There was an intergovernmental committee in the White House that was working on a psychological campaign to show the other side of this emotional issue, but the committee was not making much progress.

I became involved by suggesting on CNN that Saddam Hussein was losing the military war, but winning the propaganda war on the issue of civilian casualties. I predicted that the United States would do the wise thing and soon start releasing film that would help offset much of the Iraqi propaganda. A couple of weeks later, photography was released by the government that not only showed how little damage Baghdad had received, but showed that the Iraqis had themselves damaged a mosque and blamed it on bombing by the Coalition forces. It is not clear that my prediction that government officials would release this film had a significant impact on the decision to do so, but I received some feedback from the Pentagon indicating that my comments helped move the decision process forward.

The media can play many positive roles. One is to inform. Another is to enlighten. A third is to uplift. A fourth is to educate. A fifth is to criticize. A sixth is to help decision makers make better policy. A seventh is to encourage policy makers to become better planners, strategists, and visionaries. It seems to me that producers, anchors, reporters, guests, and military analysts need to think more seriously about the contributions they can make to the development and implementation of enlightened public policy. Criticism is a useful journalistic tool, but predictions and suggestions may be even more helpful. Criticism often causes top decision makers to become very defensive, while helpful suggestions are sometimes more readily received and acted upon.

Let me give another example from my experience on CNN where I may have had a small impact on public policy, in this case Israeli policy. I felt strongly that the Israeli government should not retaliate against Iraq for the Scud attacks. I pointed out a number of times on camera that, in my judgment, it would not be in the interest of the Israelis to do so. Early in the war, I had grave concerns that an Israeli attack on Iraq could fracture the rather delicate coalition that President Bush and Secretary of State Baker had put together.

It seemed clear to me that an act of retaliation by Israel would help only one nation, Iraq. I felt it would not enhance the foreign policy and long-term credibility of the Israeli government, and that it might lead to loss of life on the part of the Israeli military, particularly if Israeli aircraft were accidentally shot down by US or other Coalition aircraft. By restraining themselves, the Israelis could demonstrate to the world that they were moving to a higher level of maturity in the conduct of their foreign and defense policy.

I debated the Israeli Minister of Health Ehud Olmert on a live CNN hookup with Tel Aviv. Angrily, he asked how the "general" (referring to me) would feel if he were in Washington when it was being hit by Scuds. I replied that I knew what it was like to be attacked by enemy forces, pointing out that as a small boy I had witnessed the Japanese attack on Pearl Harbor. I told him (and everyone watching CNN at that moment) that I remembered the frustration all of us felt in December 1941 and in the first few months of 1942 at not being able to retaliate. I suggested that retaliation was one answer to the Israeli dilemma, but not the best answer in this case. Of course, the Israeli government did restrain itself and chose not to attack Iraq. One day, perhaps, I will find out if my arguments for restraint played any role in that decision.

Another example of the power of the media comes to mind. On the seventh day of the war, I recommended three books for viewers to read in order to better understand this war. All three books sold out by the end of that day. The publishers of these three books rushed to reprint them. In one case, *How to Defeat Saddam Hussein* went from an initial printing of 2,000 copies to a reprint order in a mass paperback edition of 600,000. The decision to mass market the book was made about the same time I labeled the book "brilliant" during my strategic analysis on January 23, 1991. There was not a direct cause-and-effect relationship between my recommendation and the numbers that were printed. However, on the front cover of the Warner Books paperback edition appeared the following phrase, "As featured on CNN." On the back cover appears the following, " 'A brilliant book'—CNN review by Major General Perry M. Smith, USAF (Ret.)." I learned later that Mel Parker, vice president and editor in chief of Warner Books, was elated by my recommendation.

17

A Day in the Life of a Military Analyst

For me, each day at CNN started early. Normally I would wake up around five AM (one PM in Saudi Arabia and Iraq) and arrive at the CNN studio before six. I needed to get there early because so often, during the night or the first hours of morning, there would be a breaking event that would require quick commentary by a military expert. And, if I got to the studio early, I could observe these breaking events, then get on the phone to the Pentagon and to my other contacts around the country for some initial reactions to the latest news. I never phoned anyone before six AM, but some of my friends and former colleagues received a call soon after that.

Sometimes, when I called these people, they were not yet aware of the latest event, so I would fill them in briefly and ask for their reactions. I would compare and contrast my reactions

127

with theirs and pick up insights, nuances, and perspectives that had not occurred to me. On occasion, they had no immediate reaction to an event, so I would try out my interpretation. They then reacted to my views. Often they would agree with me, but at other times they would say, "Now wait a minute. That doesn't sound right to me. Have you thought about this interpretation?" Or "Maybe you ought to call so-and-so about that." Or "I remember from history a similar thing happening, and this is how it came out." Or "I remember reading an article or book about that, and perhaps you might want to look at that."

Many times these early morning discussions with my friends and colleagues in the Pentagon and elsewhere resulted in their volunteering to do research for me. "You know, I can look into that," someone would say. Another might respond, "I've got a friend who would know something about that." A little later they would call me back and fill in the blanks in my knowledge. These people were extremely generous with their time and never asked for any recognition or reward. As a number of them explained to me, "Sir, what you are doing is very important. It is a privilege for me to help out a little."

Coming to work early was absolutely essential if I was to get ahead of the news and to comment knowledgeably for the rest of the day. In those early morning hours, staff writers and producers on the floor of the large news room at CNN filled me in on the events of the wee hours of the morning; they also alerted me to the best news stories in various newspapers and wire services.

During the mid and late morning hours, I was usually at the anchor desk, observing the various military briefings. I would share this duty and many others with my colleague in Washington, James Blackwell. Immediately after each briefing, our job was to react quickly, pointing out what we saw that was new, unique, very important, or simply different. Often we would note what had been left unsaid, such as the underlying messages. Why didn't they talk about this? What seems to be going on here? For instance, the briefers would often highlight the direct hits of bombs, but play down the bombs that missed the targets.

The questions that I fielded usually came from the anchors in Atlanta. Sometimes I received questions from Pentagon reporters Wolf Blitzer, Gene Randall, and, later, John Holliman or from CNN reporters in Saudi Arabia who had been sitting in on the military briefings. In most of these cases, I had no idea what questions I would be asked, and so I had no opportunity to frame my answers ahead of time. On the other hand, the Atlanta anchors or producers usually gave me some idea of the questions they would pose. In some cases I would suggest a relevant question or two. In these instances, I had a much better idea of what I was to be asked. If I did better in fielding questions from Atlanta anchors, it was because I had a few minutes to consider my answers.

After the morning briefings, I often went back to the hotel for a sandwich in my room and a short nap. I was back in the studio by two in the afternoon to react to the afternoon briefings from the Pentagon and to spend more time on the telephone getting ideas and asking questions. I also tried to answer my mail and faxes. I always returned phone calls from members of my informal brain trust. By around six-thirty or seven in the evening, I took off again for about forty-five minutes of exercise in a nearby athletic center. I always had a beeper with me in case I was needed, and the athletic center kept CNN on constantly so I could remain abreast of the news. (I often wondered, while I was working out on a rowing machine, how many other athletic centers around the world had CNN on all the time throughout the Gulf War.) Then I had supper, usually in my room, and returned to the studio by nine or nine-thirty, to be on the "Gulf Talk" show at eleven o'clock, review some of the TV tape from earlier in the day, or answer some more letters and telephone calls. I reviewed TV tape to see if I could notice any errors I might have made in my commentary. I seldom telephoned anyone after eleven PM; the exception was a few people in the Pentagon I knew were still at work. I returned to my hotel room around twelve-thirty AM and was usually asleep by one.

Each day I visited a large room on the seventh floor where younger CNN staff members answered phone calls and read and sorted the mail. There was a separate box for mail addressed to me, and I checked it at least twice a day. I found it to be very helpful to talk to these young people to find out the reactions around the country, the kinds of questions viewers were asking, and what the most emotional issues were (antiwar protesters, the televised display of downed aviators, and the Baghdad coverage were at the top of the list). I was vitally interested in what caused people to take the trouble to send letters and faxes or make phone calls.

Of course, I went to the makeup room a couple of times each day and was prepared for the camera by one of the four delightful makeup artists who pulled shifts throughout the day, night, and weekends. With my shiny head and wrinkled face, I needed lots of help.

I maintained about a four-hour sleep cycle for the six weeks. But about every four days I went to the hotel early, usually getting six or seven hours of solid sleep. Throughout the forty-two day war, I was putting in for CNN between seventeen hours and eighteen hours each day. The rest of the time was spent in exercise, eating, or sleeping. I took almost every Sunday off to return to Augusta, to spend some time with my wife and my eighty-seven-year-old mother, with Red our dog and Patches our cat, and to go to church.

I became concerned about the very long work day and the danger of getting deeper and deeper into sleep deficit. But I found it almost impossible to sleep longer than a few hours each night because of the demands of the schedule, my great interest in what was going on, and my desire not to lose touch with events. I also had sensed quite early in the war that this campaign would not last a long time. I felt that I could sustain this heavy pace of activity for a number of weeks without getting sick or becoming so tired that I would make lots of mistakes. However, if I had it to do over again, I would try to get more sleep at night and take a longer nap in the afternoon so that I could sustain my ability to comment knowledgeably for longer periods.

Over the course of the war, I made many mistakes. I learned from each one. Some of these mistakes, shortcomings, and lessons learned are worth discussing.

I clearly did not present enough in-depth perspectives. I had a lot of ideas about how I could explain aspects of this war using in-depth analyses, yet I prepared and went on camera with these analyses only five or six times. I didn't do more because I was so busy reacting to current events that I didn't have much time or energy left to write analyses, present them to Ed Turner for his comments, and deliver them on camera. I did only about one a week, while I should probably have prepared one every other day. This was a sin of omission rather than a sin of commission. I might have enhanced the reputation of CNN as a network that is interested in strategic analysis if I had been more aggressive and more energetic. Through them I might have made a more significant and lasting contribution to the education of viewers on the strategic lessons of this war and what might be learned about leadership, planning, empowerment, crisis management, and integrity under pressure.

Another error of omission was not drawing the viewers' attention to some of the grossest analytical mistakes being made on CNN and the other networks. A gross mistake repeated over and over tended to gain a level of legitimacy that I found disturbing. When CNN and the other networks were not making these corrections themselves, I felt an obligation to do so. My error lay in doing this only on one occasion. On that occasion, I went through a number of myths and tried to provide the realities.

I pointed out that many commentators missed the high-tech story. Pierre Sprey, self-employed military analyst, made some absurd comments about how high-tech could not work. He represented the antitechnology wing of the congressionally mandated Military Reform Caucus. This wing sincerely believed the military's fascination with high technology was fundamentally in error. During the Gulf War many in this wing were unwilling to admit that *they* had been in error.

Tony Cordesman pointed out on ABC that the Iraqis, by placing tanks and other military equipment inside of berms (sand walls), made it "a hundred times more difficult" for allied aircraft to destroy these vehicles. He was way off the mark. I am not sure how this idea came to him. It proved quite easy to destroy these vehicles using laser-guided five-hundred-pound bombs. In fact, putting the vehicles in berms made it easier to find them from the air.

Another mistake I made was allowing myself to be thrown

on camera to narrate incoming TV tape without demanding that I be given five or ten minutes to review it. I let the sense of urgency of each producer overcome my desire to do careful analysis. Throughout the entire war, I never once slowed down the process in the name of more thoughtful analysis. In retrospect, this was quite inexcusable.

I also made a number of technical errors. For instance, I said that the F-16 had a bombing accuracy of about forty feet (in other words, half the bombs would fall within a forty-foot radius of the target.) I was wrong. Because the F-16s were dropping bombs from an altitude above 10,000 feet in order to stay out of the range of much of the antiaircraft artillery fire and surface-to-air missiles, more than half of their bombs dropped outside a one-hundred-foot radius of the intended target.

18

The Ground Campaign

The best generals understand that the way to defeat an enemy is to defeat his strategy. Colin Powell and Norm Schwarzkopf knew exactly how to do that. They understood the importance of working on the minds of the enemy leaders. In this regard, a little word can have a powerful meaning. Such was the case as the world anticipated the ground campaign. Secretary of Defense Cheney was very careful to use "if" rather than "when" when referring to a ground war or a ground campaign. By using the phrase, "if there is a ground campaign," Cheney was sending a powerful message to Saddam Hussein; that is, the Coalition might win this war with air power alone, and Hussein could not count on a ground war where there would be many American casualties. During the war, there was a strong consensus among military intelligence officials and military experts that Saddam Hussein's strategy was to so bloody the ground forces of the Coalition that these nations would become discouraged and sue for peace. Cheney understood this well and wanted to send a key message to Saddam: You had better leave Kuwait because we will not follow your strategy by attacking on the ground in the early weeks of this war.

Cheney, Powell, and Schwarzkopf were never convinced that the war could be won by air power alone, but they were in agreement that there was no rush to commence a ground war. President Bush had been crystal clear on this issue. He demanded a strategy that minimized casualties on the side of the Coalition, and the air campaign was doing just that. General Schwarzkopf did not get into the details of the air campaign and let his air component commander implement the plan that the Checkmate team had originally developed. He was much more involved in the development of the ground campaign. Whereas General Glosson, the chief air planner, called upon the intellectual resources of the Checkmate group in the Pentagon (some of whom joined Glosson's staff in Riyadh) to assist him with his planning, General Schwarzkopf found outside assistance less helpful in planning the ground campaign. He was looking for really creative thinking, but often found "mechanistic thinking" when he asked for assistance. Hence, much of the planning he did himself with the support of his immediate staff. It was very helpful, of course, that Schwarzkopf was a serious student of warfare who, like Gen. George Patton, Jr., had read hundreds of books on military history and strategy. Unfortunately, many general officers get so caught up in their day-to-day problems, attending meetings and talking on the telephone, that they do not take much time to think about combat.

After the air campaign had been under way for a few weeks, it was clear to most members of the media that the Iraqi army, despite taking a horrible beating, was not likely to surrender to air power, so some kind of a ground campaign would be needed. There was growing interest on the part of the media about when this campaign would take place and what would be the operational concept for it.

The air campaign was continuing quite successfully, yet there were growing pressures to liberate Kuwait quickly and to end the conflict. The rape of Kuwait by Iraqi soldiers was continuing, and many Kuwaitis were becoming desperate for food. There were also humanitarian concerns about the Iraqis. Saddam's misguided leadership and the bombing of electrical generating plants as well as key roads and bridges had already caused Iraqi citizens great distress. Many observers felt that concluding this war quickly would diminish the suffering of the Iraqi people. As we all know now, the liberation of Kuwait and conclusion of the war did not end the tragedy of the Iraqi people. In fact, in many ways the situation became worse, thanks to the continued ruthlessness of Saddam Hussein.

By mid-February, the Iraqi army in Kuwait and southern Iraq was in bad shape. Thousands of Iraqi soldiers had either moved south and crossed the border into Saudi Arabia to surrender or had drifted back into Iraq as they became increasingly disconsolate after being bombed on a regular basis for over a month. Also there had been a few incidents in which individuals surrendered to helicopters. However, hundreds of thousands of Iraqi troops remained in Kuwait, and Saddam Hussein seemed unwilling to remove them.

By early February, it was clear to the media that General Schwarzkopf was preparing a ground assault. This was going to be the next big story, and the reporters in Saudi Arabia who had been cooling their heels for many weeks were anxious to cover it from start to finish. There was a great deal of grumbling on the part of the press because information about the disposition and movement of ground troops was being withheld from them by the military. Reporters were rarely allowed to visit first-line combat troops. The media pool system seemed to many reporters to have been designed to withhold information rather than provide access to good information. The large press corps in Saudi Arabia was chafing under the censorship of General Schwarzkopf.

The anticipation, interest, and concern on the part of the media, the American people, and much of the rest of the world about the commencement of the next phase of the war continued to build throughout the middle of February. The media kept probing and probing. When would the ground war commence? How would it be conducted? How long would it last?

On the advice of General Powell, President Bush set a deadline of noon on Saturday, February 23, for Iraq to get out of Kuwait. The last time Bush had set a deadline, war had commenced less than a day later, so the tension ran high throughout the world as this new deadline approached. At the time of the Saturday deadline, there was so much interest in the possibility of a new phase of the war breaking out that people who had followed CNN so closely throughout the conflict turned in even greater numbers to their CNN channel.

At noon, Saturday, February 23, there were more people in the United States watching CNN than the other three major networks combined. Ironically, CNN coverage at this time was rather weak, whereas the other networks provided excellent war coverage. The three major networks were providing commentary, graphics, and animation about the upcoming ground campaign that were of higher quality than CNN's. The people were watching CNN because they figured if there was going to be action (and ground action seemed likely to begin very soon), CNN would cover the action best. The ground war broke out that evening, and the world's attention immediately focused on it with a greater intensity than at any time since the early days of the air campaign back in mid-January.

Schwarzkopf had a strategy that included a major deception plan. He wanted to fool the Iraqi military, and he did so brilliantly by ordering a sweeping envelopment from the West and by not launching the expected amphibious attack from the Persian Gulf across the beaches of Kuwait. The best military commanders deceive their enemy in two ways: First, they make him believe that they will do something, then they don't. This approach causes the enemy to waste time, effort, and money building fortifications and deploying forces in locations that will not be attacked. The second approach is to attack from an unexpected direction. This can also be very effective, for the enemy, caught off guard, is not prepared to fight in this unanticipated area. Schwarzkopf was successful with both elements of his deception plan. In order to pull off this plan, Schwarzkopf had to fool the media, and the media thereafter felt damaged and misled. The media believed that Schwarzkopf had used (or misused) the press and the correspondents. Many did not realize that deception planning in wartime has been a legitimate activity for centuries.

The next hundred hours proved very dramatic, but CNN did not cover this story well. The other networks generally managed to get their reporters into Kuwait more quickly than CNN, establish good satellite links, and feed footage back to their studios in the United States. The lesson here may be that when there is time to get ready, and for short periods of time, the three major networks can compete favorably with CNN on war coverage. CNN probably would have regained dominance in depth and breadth of coverage if the ground campaign had lasted many weeks.

There are a number of lessons that can be drawn from the ground campaign. First, there may be no better example in military history of a commander "preparing the battlefield." In fact, this thirty-eight-day air campaign against tactical targets in Kuwait and southern Iraq went beyond "preparing the battlefield." It was an example of the "destruction of a battlefield." The second lesson is the value of surprise, which has already been discussed. The third lesson of the war is the reaffirmation of the principle of war, "mass," the use of heavy concentrations of military power with overpowering firepower, decisiveness, and aggressiveness.

Schwarzkopf gets high marks for successfully carrying out a sustained air campaign and also for conducting a ground campaign that in some ways was equally impressive. Although the air campaign was decisive and the ground campaign was, to a very large extent, a mopping-up operation, that's exactly what the President, Schwarzkopf, and the American people wanted.

The technological marvels of the air forces of all the various services were duplicated by the ground forces. The M-1 tank, the Bradley infantry fighting vehicle, the multiple-launch rocket system, and the armed helicopters all worked well. Perhaps the greatest weakness on the ground was the inability of the artillery of the Coalition nations to keep up with the fast moving tanks, armored personnel carriers, and other vehicles.

Although one hundred hours of ground combat against a

weakened enemy is not a very demanding test, there was enough combat for many tactics and doctrines to be tried on the ultimate proving ground. There were some military leaders who would have wished for a longer period of ground combat against a tougher foe, but the vast majority of the viewing audience were pleased with the brevity of the campaign and the unexpectedly low number of casualties.

19

Smart Bombs and Dumb Bombs

Just after Kuwait was liberated a fascinating question arose: How accurate had the bombs and missiles been? An unverified report in the *Washington Post* from a "senior official in the Pentagon" indicated that 70 percent of the bombs missed their targets. Many journalists pointed out that the precision-guided bombs and missiles ("smart" bombs and missiles) were remarkably accurate, but the "dumb" bombs, or bombs that did not have terminal guidance systems, missed their targets most of the time.

Among some reporters there was a "trading of ignorances." They failed to understand that bombs are like hand grenades: to come close to the target can still produce impressive results. The measure of merit for bombing is very much like the measure of merit for artillery: Was the target destroyed? It is not: Did every round hit every target?

But there is another aspect to this issue of bombs missing targets. When someone uses a shotgun to down a skeet disk, a couple of hundred pellets fly up toward the target. If four or five pellets strike the target and the skeet disk disintegrates, no one seems to mind that ninety-five percent of the pellets missed the target. Again, the compelling issue is: Was the target destroyed? For instance, I have never seen a headline in the sports pages along the following lines: "Jones Wins Skeet Tournament With a Perfect Score, but 95% of Pellets Miss the Target."

To cite a specific example, let's examine an aircraft, the F-16, which flew tens of thousands of bombing sorties during the Gulf War. The F-16 drops bombs by rolling in at high altitude, diving down at about a 40 degree dive angle and releasing bombs that have no terminal guidance system. In other words, F-16s drop dumb bombs. F-16s dropping unguided bombs have a circular error probable of forty feet in peacetime (half the bombs fall within a circle with a radius of forty feet). In order to stay above most of the antiaircraft artillery fire in the Gulf War, the F-16 pilots released their bombs at a higher altitude than they had practiced in peacetime (from twelve thousand feet rather than from six thousand feet). Hence, half the bombs were missing by more than one hundred feet in combat.

There is nothing new about this lack of perfect accuracy. The reason that bombs have big warheads and that bombers carry lots of them is that bombs have always missed targets. All knowledgeable military aviators understand that the vast majority of unguided bombs will miss a given target. But since air planners had always intended to drop more than one unguided bomb against important targets in order to destroy the target, the miss factor was hardly unexpected.

There was a benefit, of course, when members of the media raised this issue. It gave the military a chance to educate the reading and viewing public on air doctrine, targeting philosophy, and the realities of air combat. In fairness to the media critics, they did identify, albeit indirectly, a major lesson from this war. Precision-guided bombs, even though considerably more expensive than unguided bombs, make great good sense. Far fewer bombs are needed, and the chance of damage to civilian areas is minimized, if precision-guided bombs are used. The prewar argument that dumb bombs (unguided after release from the aircraft) on smart airplanes (like the F-16) were almost as good as smart bombs (guided after release) on smart airplanes did not hold up. Although aircraft like the F-16 have excellent bombing systems, and are therefore labeled smart airplanes, these systems are not good enough if the pilot is going to release his bombs at high altitude. The bomb falls so far after release and is so affected by the wind or by a small error in the release parameters that the bomb will miss, often by more than one hundred feet. In future wars, instead of 10 percent of bombs being precision guided, I would expect a much higher percentage.

The B-52, which is another aircraft that drops dumb bombs, did so with much greater accuracy than it did in the Vietnam War. But it was still "carpet bombing." The strategic bomber in the future, whether it is a B-52, B-1, or B-2, will continue to have a capability to drop nonnuclear bombs, but these bombs will probably be precision-guided bombs. Carpet bombing using dumb bombs, which has been such an important part of warfare since World War I, is a tactic of the past. Good riddance! This bombing technique has cost over a million lives and two million casualties. Most of these deaths and casualties in past wars have been civilian.

The new paradigm of precision should impact all the military services for the next few years. But military planners must look beyond the use of bombs and missiles to precisely attack targets. Technology may soon allow the destruction of key elements of a military target without killing soldiers or totally destroying the target. If an enemy tank can be rendered ineffective by preventing the engine from operating or by ruining the gun-firing computers, winning wars through means that are largely nonlethal may be possible.

The implications of these developments could be profound in both positive and negative ways. Despite all the advantages, this capability could make the resort to war an easier choice for national leaders. Hence, as these new technologies are explored, many issues need to be examined by political leaders, military planners, war gamers, ethicists, and members of the media.

Women and the War

Women were used in the Gulf War in combat support activities that put many at risk. That may turn out to be the most important aspect of the entire conflict, especially when one considers the domestic and the international implications. The press focused a lot of attention on the issue of women in combat during the Desert Shield buildup period. From August 2, 1990, until January 16, 1991, many women soldiers, airmen and marines and a few from the navy were interviewed by the press. The press took note of how many American military women were in the Persian Gulf area (over thirty-two thousand) and the kinds of jobs they held. Most were in combat support, as helicopter pilots, or combat service support positions, as supply officers and noncommissioned officers, communications specialists, and maintenance personnel. However, it appeared that many would be in harm's way when enemy missiles, bombs, and artillery began to fly. There was also a danger of death from friendly fire in the heat of combat. Although there had been some exploration of this issue in the aftermath of the Panama invasion—a few women had engaged in combatlike activities there—now there were many months available for a deeper examination of this issue.

Substantive interviews of women examined the nature of their jobs, how they held up in the tough desert conditions, and their views on the issue of women in combat. It was clear to viewers that most of these women were well trained and well motivated and willing to take on the rigors and dangers of combat if called upon to do so.

Immediately after the Gulf War, there was a movement in the United States Congress to authorize women, by law, to participate in combat activities related to flying combat aircraft. Congresswoman Pat Shroeder, a long-term member of the House Armed Services Committee, led the charge on this issue. Schroeder has felt for years that by not allowing women to participate in combat, military women were being denied a full opportunity for promotion. They couldn't compete equally with men because they were not allowed to hold the jobs that would make them top contenders for rapid promotion to the higher ranks.

In late April 1991, the Defense Advisory Committee on Women in the Services recommended to the Bush administration that all legal restrictions on the role of servicewomen be lifted. Just two weeks later, on May 8, in a voice vote, the House Armed Services Committee voted to allow women to serve in combat aircraft in the air force, navy, and marines. This step, if it is sustained by the full House and Senate (which I think is quite likely) would be momentous. There is an enormous drive now to break down the last barriers to giving women the opportunity to engage in combat. There is no legal restriction on women in combat roles in the army, but as a matter of policy women have been precluded from flying attack helicopters or from serving in combat roles in the infantry, armor, engineeers or field artillery. If the other services allow women to fly combat aircraft, which now is quite likely, the army will feel great pressure to remove its policy restrictions on combat roles also.

The implications are profound. First of all, it means that the composition of the United States military should be more broadly based. Whereas, in the past, women had characteristically comprised no more than 12 percent of the overall military population in the United States, there is little reason why that percentage shouldn't become considerably higher. This means that the job of recruiting young people into the military should be easier than it has ever been in the past.

Other trends will also be at work in the postwar period. The military will shrink considerably in size in the future. In addition, with women serving in combat roles, the possibility of their getting promoted to higher levels will become much better. Men will still have a bit of an edge over women in promotion to the highest ranks for many years, but that edge will narrow considerably as women obtain jobs, such as commanders of combat units, that will make them more competitive at the various promotion boards. At the moment, the highest rank that a woman can expect to achieve is major general, and very few have ever made that rank in the past. In the immediate future lieutenant general will become attainable for women, and sometime after the turn of the century the four-star rank of general should also be open to a few women.

Significantly, of course, 108 nations were watching CNN and were exposed to these kinds of issues and interviews, so this war was a major step forward in the women's rights movement, both in the United States and around the world. I am sure that there are men in many nations who are appalled to see how far the United States has proceeded on this issue. On the other hand, many others would cheer this evolution toward a new equal opportunity trend within the American armed forces.

KC-10s with massive loads of jet fuel refueled aircraft of many types from many nations. This picture shows an F-15 from the First Tactical Fighter Wing at Langley Air Force Base, Virginia, being refueled. The F-15s played two important but quite different roles. The F-15C and F-15D provided air cover and shot down Iraqi aircraft while the F-15E dropped bombs on key targets. (photo courtesy of Department of Defense Public Affairs)

As the ground war became imminent, Saddam Hussein ordered hundreds of Kuwait oil rigs set on fire. The pollution of the air in the region became an environmental disaster. (photo courtesy of Department of Defense Public Affairs)

The Big Three. Secretary of Defense Dick Cheney, Chairman of the Joint Chiefs of Staff Colin Powell and Commander in Chief of the Central Command H. Norman Schwarzkopf. By permitting Schwarzkopf to plan and carry out the war, Cheney and Powell established themselves in the eyes of the world as extraordinary leaders. They gained great respect by their willingness to give power away. (photo courtesy of Department of Defense Public Affairs)

Women served in the combat zone in many capacities: as military police, as pilots of support helicopters and tanker and cargo aircraft, and as commanders of supply, communications and other support units. (photo courtesy of Department of Defense Public Affairs)

The battleship *Wisconsin*, commissioned more than forty years ago, firing its 16-inch guns at Iraqi ground positions in Kuwait. The two-thousand-pound projectiles have a range of twenty miles and are quite accurate. (photo courtesy of Department of Defense Public Affairs)

The famous stealth fighter as it lands after a combat mission over Iraq. This radar-invisible aircraft (F-117) dropped the first bombs on military targets in Baghdad. Throughout the war these aircraft, flying at night, dropped precision-guided two-thousand-pound bombs on key targets, mostly in and around Baghdad. No-F117s were hit by enemy fire in flights over the most heavily defended areas in Iraq. (photo courtesy of Department of Defense Public Affairs)

Lt. Gen. Charles Horner, United States Air Force. Horner was the air component commander for General Schwarzkopf. He and his staff planned and executed the entire air campaign. Horner received assistance from the Pentagon Checkmate brain trust. (photo courtesy of Department of Defense Public Affairs).

The Iraqi defenses in Kuwait City. A graphic reminder of why Schwarzkopf chose not to launch an amphibious attack across the beaches of Kuwait. (photo courtesy of Department of Defense Public Affairs)

Christiane Amanpour, the CNN heroine of Baghdad. Her tough-minded willingness to press the limits of Iraqi censorship impressed many viewers. (photo courtesy of CNN)

One way to eliminate the danger of land mines. This is an M-728 combat engineer vehicle from the 24th Armored Infantry Division. (photo courtesy of Department of Defense Public Affairs)

Saddam Hussein hoped that these hardened aircraft shelters would protect his air force from attack. Special steel-encased two-thousand-pound precision-guided bombs were able to penetrate these tough shelters. (photo courtesy of Department of Defense Public Affairs)

Hundreds of aircraft shelters were attacked by precision-guided bombs. The result was the destruction of that portion of the Iraqi air force that did not get shot down or escape to Iran. (photo courtesy of Department of Defense Public Affairs)

Iraqi troops by the tens of thousands tried to escape from Kuwait just as the ground campaign began. They were stopped by air and ground power. These vehicles were trying to escape through the Mutla pass, north of Kuwait City. The white building in the background is the Mutla police station. (photo courtesy of Department of Defense Public Affairs).

An Iraqi tank that didn't get away. (photo courtesy of Department of Defense Public Affairs).

Charles Jaco's dramatic reports out of Saudi Arabia during Scud attacks and out of Kuwait City as it was being liberated made him an instant hero to many viewers. The flow of favorable mail into CNN about Jaco was huge. (photo courtesy of CNN)

This caption and the dramatic music of CNN during the war became imbedded in the minds of a billion people worldwide. (photo courtesy of CNN)

21

Military Lessons of the War

The six-weeks war of 1991 moved rapidly and at a pace that was much quicker than what most people had expected. It was hard for anyone to draw significant lessons while the war was going on. However, now that we can examine the war in its totality, there are a number of factors that have changed the face of warfare, the course of international relations, and the way the news media may conduct themselves in future wars and crises. In this chapter I will discuss the military lessons of the war. Only by understanding the military lessons can the reader fully understand the media lessons of the war.

As far as warfare itself is concerned, there were a number of significant paradigm shifts. The first was in the area of technology. For the very first time, technical sophistication combined with excellent reliability to make extraordinary precision achievable. The paradigm of precision was accomplished. Military targets could be struck quite easily, using a small number of bombs and missiles. In addition, civilian casualties could be reduced to a bare minimum, since these precision weapons seldom strayed off course. Almost as dramatic as the accuracy of these weapons is the reliability of these highly complex systems, even in the stress of combat.

As far as this important issue of reliability is concerned, a useful analogy is the quartz wristwatch. I wear a digital watch that tells time in various formats and has three alarms, a stopwatch, and the storage capacity for twenty telephone numbers. It is an inexpensive watch that would cost less than fifty dollars today. For a time I had a faulty watch band and I dropped the watch on the ground at least ten times while I was jogging, yet the watch has never broken. I have had to replace the battery only twice in five years. This watch is certainly much more complex than the old wind-up watch that told time but did nothing else. In comparative terms, the watch I wear today is the least expensive watch I have ever had, and yet it is the first watch I have owned that has never had to be fixed or cleaned. It is a much more sophisticated watch, but it's also much, much more reliable.

The same maturation of technology pertains to the high-tech weaponry that we saw in operation in the 1991 Gulf War. Let me give a perspective from my personal experience as an airman. In 1968 and 1969 I flew the F-4 Phantom, the principal American fighter of the Vietnam War. Employed in combat by both the navy and air force from 1965 through 1972, it engaged in missions to attack targets in North Vietnam, Laos, Cambodia, and South Vietnam. The F-4 was a fine aircraft for its time, but there were many of things about this supersonic fighter that were rather unreliable and difficult to deal with. For instance, in order to replace the radio in the F-4D model, you had to remove the rear ejection seat. This meant that if a radio failed, the pilot and his weapons systems officer, who manned the back seat of this two-man aircraft, would have to sit on the ground for a couple of hours while a new radio was installed. To change a radio in the more modern F-15 takes less than five minutes. The maintenance technician just opens up three fasteners, lifts up a panel door in the nose of the aircraft, slides the old radio out and shoves in the new one. It is a quick and easy operation.

The radar in the F-4, which was used in combat both to

shoot down enemy aircraft and to drop bombs, caused us trouble about once in every four combat missions. The radar would be either completely inoperable or seriously degraded. In comparison, the F-15 radar will cause trouble during one mission out of every fifteen. Yet the F-15 radar is much more capable and more sophisticated than the radar on the F-4. It's a "look down, shoot down" radar that has a "clean scope." This radar automatically screens out terrain features so that it doesn't pick up any stationary ground features like mountains and buildings (commonly known by the aviators as ground clutter when they appear on a radar scope) that would make finding a low-flying enemy aircraft more difficult. Compared to the F-4 radar, the F-15 radar is also easier to read, has a much longer range, and discriminates friend from foe much better.

The F-4 is a 1960s airplane, the F-15 a 1970s airplane. So, in just one decade, the air force and its contractors produced an airplane that is more capable, more reliable, more fun to fly, and much more likely to come out the victor in air-to-air combat. The F-15 costs more than the F-4, but when reliability, accuracy, and performance in combat are factored in, the newer F-15 is much cheaper than the F-4. Just to underscore the central point, higher technology does not necessarily result in lower operational rates or more difficult maintenance. To the contrary, many of the newer and more sophisticated systems, like the F-15 and the F-16, are easier to maintain and more reliable in operation.

Another impressive feature of the Gulf War was the speed of innovation. When air planners realized that the tanks, armored personnel carriers, and artillery in the Kuwaiti theater of operations were being placed inside sand berms and partially buried in sand, they quickly realized that the Maverick missile might not be the best ordnance to use against these vehicles. The Maverick has a small warhead, so a near miss under these conditions would do little good. An old idea was reexamined. Why not drop bombs on these tanks? This was something that had been discussed for many years, but the idea had always been discounted; unguided bombs just weren't accurate enough to be effective against heavily armored vehicles, since a direct hit was needed.

This time, however, a new approach was suggested. Take a

five-hundred-pound bomb, put a laser nose and some steerable fins on it, and use the same precision system that was working so well with two-thousand-pound bombs that were damaging bridges and command centers. A five-hundred-pound bomb is not very expensive. A bomb costs about a dollar per pound, so the five-hundred-pound basic bomb costs about five hundred dollars. When you put the laser kit on the nose and add the movable fins and the guidance system (which takes the laser signal and tells the fins to move in the proper ways), the overall cost rises to about nine thousand dollars. A single nine-thousand-dollar bomb destroying a Russian-built T-72 tank that costs a million dollars constitutes an excellent economic bargain for an air-power nation that has many laser designators and laser-guided bombs.

Here is a good example of a high-tech system, the laser-guided bomb, knocking out an expensive weapons system at very low cost. In the future, we should see similar high-tech developments that, in comparative terms, will be quite inexpensive. This is another shift relating to technology, the widespread availability of cheap and reliable high tech.

Logistics exemplifies another major shift in contemporary warfare. In all past conflicts, when a nation or a coalition of nations tried to fight seven or eight thousand miles from home, it was confronted with a logistical nightmare. Logistics, of course, consists of both the supply and distribution of goods. To be effective in combat, a commander must have what he needs (manpower, weapons, food, water, fuel, etc.) at the place and at the time it is needed. To handle this distribution problem, the United States and its Coalition partners needed huge numbers of ships, airplanes, and trucks.

The United States has a massive airlift capacity. In addition, all large cargo aircraft of the US Air Force have a built-in capability to refuel while airborne, enabling them to reach destinations halfway around the world without stopping at airfields along the way. This air-refueling capability considerably enhances the ability to get troops into combat areas fast and to resupply them there. The United States Air Force today has more than six-hundred large tanker aircraft. These aircraft provide more air-refueling capability than all the rest of the world combined.

In addition, the United States has built a number of fast sea-lift ships, ships that sail not at twelve knots but at twenty-five or thirty knots, so they can move supplies twice as fast as in previous wars. There is a shortage of these fast sea-lift ships, but with adequate funding this shortage could be reduced significantly over the next few years. This combination of fast sea-lift and airlift and air-refueling aircraft gives the United States an awesome logistics capability.

Although Secretary of Defense Robert McNamara denied it, the United States military had a serious bomb shortage in the Vietnam War. The best weapon with which to attack a specific target was often not loaded on a combat aircraft because the bomb was not available on the base or on the aircraft carrier. In the Gulf War, where the intensity of bombing was very high, logistics was always a challenge, but never a major limitation. Prior to the outbreak of hostilities, the United States had stockpiled large quantities of materiel in the area, and a flow pattern for subsequent resupply was a major part of our victory. One can argue that by the spring of 1991 the United States had established itself as the dominant military power in the world, given its ability to fight a war from a great distance while overcoming logistical difficulties.

A third major shift was in the area of leadership. Now that the Pentagon has great command, control, and communications facilities, ensuring instantaneous access to our forces around the world, many felt that all wars would be controlled by the Pentagon itself. Recent history has taught us that a leader who has the means to control a crisis situation from a central location has had a tendency to do just that. Yet in the Gulf War just the opposite happened. High Pentagon officials had the opportunity to micromanage the war, but chose not to do so. In other words, the commander in the field was given power, and he used it brilliantly. Schwarzkopf proved to be a self-confident, decisive commander who relished the chance to take charge. A weaker commander might have checked back with the Pentagon so often that he would have incrementally relinquished power and returned it to the chairman of the Joint Chiefs of Staff and the secretary of defense. The lesson here is clear: pick strong leaders, empower them, give them support, and the results should provide success. Schwarzkopf became an American hero, while Colin Powell and Dick Cheney enhanced their stature by giving power away.

In the past, before the days of instant communications, field commanders had a great deal of autonomy. Now we see autonomy reestablished by conscious choice of wise senior leaders. Combined with good staff support from the Pentagon, a breakthrough occurred. The central headquarters supported the field commander but did not micromanage him.

In the wake of the Gulf War many people are beginning to examine and analyze the military and its leadership, its empowering techniques, its use of analysis and technology, and its nurturing skills. This experience should be useful not only to future military leaders from many nations, but to corporations, foundations, hospitals, universities, and other large institutions that are looking for ways to empower their lower level leaders so that they can take and carry out decisions without constantly checking with their bosses. In the business world, a good analogy would be the 3M Company, which empowers its division chiefs to develop and market new products with little guidance from the top. The work of the corporate staff is to assist rather than micromanage the various divisions of 3M. CNN itself provides another example. I was struck by the similarities in the relationships between Powell and Schwarzkopf and Tom Johnson and Ed Turner of CNN. I am finding myself using the Gulf War experience to illustrate enlightened leadership in my speeches and seminars.

A second major aspect of returning military leadership to a more traditional model involved the rediscovery of the tradition of integrity among military professionals in combat situations. It seems to me that Schwarzkopf became a model of integrity for leaders of the future, again from any field of endeavor. Schwarzkopf understood, both intuitively and from experience, that it is much better to tell the truth. Truth has a legitimacy, a coherency, and a dignity that is very powerful. This approach had a positive impact on the soldiers, sailors, airmen, and marines under General Schwarzkopf's command. I said early in the war that generals Powell and Schwarzkopf would impress us in many ways. Their sustained commitment to integrity was probably their greatest strength.

Psychological warfare is an important part of the story of the Gulf War, but the story is complex. There was success on the one hand, and failure on the other. Psychological warfare is the use of information, persuasion, and propaganda to get the enemy to take action or actions voluntarily that will help your cause. Tactical psychological warfare was directed at the combat troops in the Kuwaiti theater of operations. Using leaflets dropped by the tens of millions over frontline positions, the Coalition leaders hoped to get soldiers to abandon their equipment. The message was very simple. Your tanks, armored personnel carriers, and artillery are going to be attacked. If you want to survive, leave your equipment and move a few hundred yards away and dig a deep foxhole. To a very considerable degree the leaflet program worked, and the lives of many frontline Iraqi soldiers were saved as a result.

What was not tried was strategic psychological warfare, where Iraqi commanders in Kuwait might have been encouraged to march their troops out of Kuwait to save them from destruction and to use them to overthrow Saddam. Although this approach might have failed, it was never tried. Perhaps an opportunity was lost as a result.

What do all these military lessons mean for the media? Clearly, leaders of various television and radio networks, of newspapers and magazines, and professors of journalism need to address a fundamental question: How are they to deal with paradigm shifts? Why did it take so many members of the media until 1991 to recognize and report on the profound technological improvement in military weapons that began in earnest in the late 1970s? The reason seems rather clear. The media, to a large extent, are captives of their own culture and beliefs. They have been caught in a classic case of "group think" about the military. This view maintains that government and military officials cannot be trusted and always try to manipulate the news in their favor. The military for a decade had been saying that high technology and reliability could go hand in hand. The military was correct, but much of the media seemed unable or unwilling to grasp this reality in the early days of the Gulf War.

Every media organization like every military organization needs to spend some time, intellectual energy, and money on overcoming "group think." I have confidence that after a period when the media decry the censorship of the Pentagon and General Schwarzkopf, it will undertake to discard its outdated viewpoint and report on the military from a new, more healthy, and more realistic perspective.

22

Parallel Transformations in Warfare and in News Reporting

The Gulf War has changed the course of history in two very significant ways. Warfare will never again be conducted the way it was in the past as long as one or more of the combatant nations have modern weapons. It is already quite clear that the ability to deliver munitions with great accuracy will change the tactics, doctrine, strategy, and morality of warfare.

This war has also changed the way the media will cover future crises and combat. This war has firmly established the primary role of twenty-four-hour television news networks in times of emergencies, natural disasters, crises, and war. People now expect that information will be provided them on an instantaneous and continuous basis for the duration of the crisis. At any hour of the day or night vast numbers of viewers want to be able to flip on their televisions and find crisp, vigorous, critical, and instantaneous coverage of major crises and wars. The Gulf War helped to establish the model. That model is CNN.

Let us first examine how the military will change in the future. Air power has become a more important factor in warfare than it has ever been in the past. Back in the 1920s and 1930s such prominent air-power theorists as the Italian Giulio Douhet, the Englishman Lord Hugh M. Trenchard, and the American Billy Mitchell conceived of air power as the decisive force in warfare. Douhet developed his theories in his seminal book *The Command of the Air*, first published in 1921. He argued that air power in future warfare would not only be the predominant force, but would change warfare forever. Douhet, who would be labeled a futurist today, took a long-range look at military forces and concluded that eventually there would be very little requirement for naval or ground forces. Under the Douhet thesis, the nation with the weaker air-combat capability would be so heavily bombarded that it would soon give up. People's morale would break down under such bombardment, he theorized, and national leaders would act quickly to end further devastation.

Douhet's theories were considered extremely radical for the 1920s, when airpower was still in its infancy. He argued that air power alone would become the primary military factor in power relationships among nations. In fact, Douhet postulated that nations would not go to war when it was clear that one nation was much stronger in air power than another, simply because the weaker nation would realize capitulation was the only choice available.

A more sophisticated and more humane approach was taken by air planners in the United States at the Army Air Corps Tactical School, which was first established at Langley Field in Virginia in the early 1920s and later moved to Maxwell Field in Alabama. An impressive amount of intellectual effort and energy went into inventing this new doctrine of the United States Army Air Corps. In the 1960s, I wrote a book about postwar planning accomplished by the Army Air Corps during World War II (*The Air Force Plans for Peace: 1943–1945*). During my research, I closely examined the development of United States air doctrine during the 1930s. These early air planners believed the United States needed to develop a capability for precision strategic bombardment if air power were to predominate.

While Douhet had suggested the massive bombing of cities would kill tens of thousands of people, the Air Corps Tactical School advocated attacking very precisely a few specific key industries within a nation in order to bring the war economy of that nation to its knees. An example was ball-bearing production. If the United States could knock out the small number of ball-bearing factories in Nazi Germany, it was suggested, the German economy would literally and figuratively grind to a halt. The Germans would not have ball bearings for their tanks, truck engines, and industrial machines. Within a short period of time, probably a matter of months, their war machine would deteriorate so significantly that they would have to surrender.

In order to have this bombardment campaign succeed, however, a nation needed the capability to drop bombs very precisely. Secretly, the United States developed the Norden bomb sight for the specific purpose of giving bombers the capability of hitting targets with great accuracy. Despite these impressive conceptual and technological efforts, the precision bombardment campaign over Germany in World War II proved a failure. The Norden bomb sight did not provide enough accuracy, especially in bad weather.

However, there was another major factor that significantly contributed to this failure. The air planners did not take fully into account the economic principle of substitution. If the Americans and British knocked out all the ball-bearing plants in Germany, the Germans could still buy ball bearings from a neutral country such as Sweden. The Swedes made very good ball bearings, and they were willing to sell them to the Germans.

So there were two fundamental problems with employing the strategy of precision bombardment developed by the Air Corps Tactical School. One was not having the technology for precision bombing, and the other was the inability to prevent the enemy from finding substitute products or substitute sources of supply. Nevertheless these prescient air planners of the 1930s were on to something very important. Sometime in the future, a nation might develop bombing accuracies down to a few feet and a targeting strategy that took into account both the military and economic factors in warfare. This is what happened in the Gulf War as air power became the dominant military force.

These developments took many years and many wars to fully evolve. Toward the end of the Vietnam War, it had become clear that precision delivery of munitions could be achieved. Laser-guided bombs were, in fact, used with excellent results in the latter part of that conflict, as were bombs guided by electrical-optical (television) systems. The American defense industry, working closely with the various military services, further improved this technology over the years. By the time the Gulf War commenced, systems were ready, the training was excellent, and the targeting philosophy in place. In short, all four services of the United States military establishment were prepared to conduct an air campaign based on the precise delivery of bombs and missiles throughout the day and night, in good and marginal weather conditions.

In parallel with the military preparations for war were the preparations by the media to cover the war. As the crisis escalated, so did the news coverage by all the television and radio networks and by the vast print media. The following chapter explains how CNN gained and maintained the upper hand in television coverage of the war. By working hard to report the news of the war as completely as possible, every minute of the day, CNN influenced to some degree all the major elements of the media.

In a short speech in Washington, D.C., that I delivered two weeks after Kuwait was liberated, I offered the provocative point that the center of international media is no longer in New York, London, Washington, Tokyo, or Paris. It is in Atlanta, Georgia. When the chief military correspondent for CBS spends the day watching CNN and when newspaper reporters from around the world write their stories while watching CNN, the way the news is reported to the world has changed dramatically. A shift of major proportions has taken place among the media of the world. CNN more than any other organization has led this transformation. How did CNN manage this coup? The next chapter tries to explain.

23

Making It Work: Some Key People at CNN

The phenomenon of CNN is, in large part, the result of the sustained efforts of Ed Turner, the executive vice president, who has been with CNN from its start in 1980. He is a soft-spoken, modest man who listens well, is "tuned in" to new ideas, encourages innovation, and is very creative. Whereas Ted Turner was seldom seen in the CNN studio in Atlanta during the Gulf War, Ed Turner was there throughout.

During the Gulf War, Ed Turner was battered by criticism from many directions. The most severe denunciations concerned Peter Arnett's coverage from Baghdad. But Ed Turner was also criticized for too much "breathless journalism" and too much "quickie" stuff put on the air without a strategic perspective and sound analysis. Some of this criticism was valid. Turner took these thoughtful and constructive comments very well. Some of the comments, however, were unfair. These were often based on professional jealousy as other segments of the media watched CNN win and hold such a wide audience. These were harder on Turner.

He lived in the Omni Hotel throughout the six-week war so he had his hand on the pulse of the operation. He came to work early and worked late. I was working seventeen- and eighteen-hour days and there were days when he worked longer hours than I did.

Tom Johnson, the president of CNN, also played an important role. He has been with CNN for only a short time, coming to Atlanta in the summer of 1990 from the Times Mirror organization. He spent a lot of time in the news area, talking to people, listening, and seeking out their ideas. He even provided a complimentary, twenty-four-hour-a-day, informal buffet for CNN employees in Atlanta throughout most of the war. They were working such long hours in such a frantic environment that having food available at all times was a practical touch that we all appreciated.

The team of Ed Turner and Tom Johnson provided CNN a steady hand of quiet competence. They are both very strong in their listening skills, and their leadership came through very well during the six-week period. They worked their people very hard and didn't pay them very much; yet throughout the Gulf War the staff always seemed to be in high spirits. Each group of CNN employees played important roles: the anchors, the producers, the bookers, the staff writers, the reporters.

The anchors play the vital role of capturing the attention and the interest of the viewers. Each CNN anchor must be flexible and deal well with chaos and many changes. They must talk and still listen through their earpiece when a producer is giving them new directions. When there is total pandemonium and confusion as they prepare to go on camera, they sometimes get piqued and, on occasion, grouse at producers and others. Let me give the flavor of some of the complaints to producers that I heard from the anchor desk: "I am on in twenty seconds and I don't have a *clue* as to what is happening." "I have two producers telling me two different things; *please* make up your mind." The anchor comment I liked most was, "Well, we can toss to the general; he always has something to say."

I was fascinated with how much profanity the producers use and how little there is from the anchors. The anchors seem to feel that if they get into the habit of using bad language, they might slip up on camera. Incidentally, there was some profanity on camera at CNN during the war, but it was usually when Scud missiles were en route and a reporter in Saudi Arabia was under great stress.

Being an anchor, it seems to me, requires a certain kind of person—someone who is bright, well educated, eclectic in his or her interests, and attractive. Anchors must read consistently well and have a pleasing voice. Being an anchor also requires a great deal of self-discipline; anchors are captives of the time-lines, the schedules worked out by the producers, and the text being produced by the writers. The opportunities for real creativity at the anchor desk are rather limited. There are times, however, particularly during interviews, when the need for follow-up questions can, in fact, allow that creativity to flow.

Because there are so many anchors at CNN, more than twenty, and because their schedules rotate, there are no anchors who are prima donnas; at least I found none in Atlanta, where most of them are located. Incipient prima donnas at CNN may find their work schedules adjusted in such a way that they have less opportunity for camera time or they might find themselves on the two AM to five AM shift. Low pay rates for anchors at CNN may also help to keep them from becoming too carried away with their own importance.

CNN is not an anchor's network, but a producer's and news gatherer's network. In fact, there was a saying at CNN before the war that CNN was the network of the generic anchor. In other words, there were no superstar anchors, and with so many CNN anchors, none was particularly well known. However, with so many people having watched CNN so many hours in a day during the war, the era of the generic CNN anchor may be over. I sat at the anchor desk for many hours every day as I watched briefings and awaited my chance to comment. Hence, I watched the anchors closely as they worked their magic on camera. Let me highlight a few CNN anchors.

Molly McCoy was usually at the anchor desk early in the morning. She has an intensity in her delivery, and it is easy to get caught up in her enthusiasm. She asks very crisp, short, and direct questions, and she also has a great deal of personal charm. She has Scandinavian looks, the high cheekbones and large blue eyes that so many people find very attractive. But it is the character of her work, her professionalism and the sharpness of her questions, that most impressed me. When I told McCoy, the day I left CNN, that I was writing a book on CNN and the war and would give my candid analysis of some of the anchors, reporters, and producers, I asked her what I should write about Molly McCoy. She quickly replied, "How about brilliant and beautiful?" I bow to her good judgment. Molly McCoy is both brilliant and beautiful.

Bobbie Battista is probably the best known of all the anchors in Atlanta. She has about her a certain mystery that seems to capture and hold the viewing audience. She may be the most intellectually curious of the anchors I dealt with. Off camera, we had long discussions about where this war was going and what it all meant. I could always count on her to ask a good initial question and to follow up with appropriate direct questions. Some of the very best on-camera dialogue I had during the war was with the very bright Bobbie Battista. I uncovered a crazy story about her life when she was an anchor in Raleigh, North Carolina. As a lark, she agreed to jump out of a large fake cake to surprise an ardent fan at his birthday party. (She was fully clothed at the time.) When I kidded her about it, she showed a fine ability to laugh at herself.

Patrick Greenlaw was the first person to interview me after the war began. A very large and outgoing man, Greenlaw reminds me of the big brother every kid would like to have to provide protection if he ever gets into trouble with the local bully. Greenlaw loves to laugh and he loves to talk. His questions were consistently good, although at times they seemed a bit longer than they needed to be. One of the vice presidents of CNN told me that Greenlaw was superb whenever he was asked on short notice to cut away from one story and go to another that was more important. He made these tough transitions with a real flair as he explained to the viewers why this interruption and abrupt transition was taking place. Also, Greenlaw was very perceptive on the first night of the war when he asked about an air campaign followed by a mopping-up ground operation. He is a very bright, engaging, fun-loving fellow.

Donna Kelly is exactly what she seems to be to the viewer—a very warm, attractive, and caring person, very appreciative of the work of others, easy to work with on the set, kind to the staff members at every level, very professional. Those who are cynical about media people and think they are too well paid, arrogant, and too carried away with their own sense of importance should get to know Donna, a sweet and thoughtful person.

Catherine Crier is well known throughout television land because of the publicity that occurred at the time of her selection as a CNN anchor. Her professional background was as a trial lawyer and later a judge. She moved directly from the legal profession to become an anchor on CNN. She is Scandinavian in her looks, with very chiseled features. Crier is sharp intellectually, broad in her view. One night, in the makeup room, she told me that being an anchor at CNN was not unlike being a lawyer. You have to put the case together quickly, to make sense of it, and to explain it to a jury (or a viewing audience) that may not have much expertise in the area. You have to ask tough questions, the right questions, and you have to move quickly. I think she is correct in these assessments. I noted, however, some discomfort at CNN because Catherine Crier had not worked her way up through the television system. She had never served as a cub reporter in a small town or as an anchor in a medium-sized town. This seemed to lead, at times, to a bit of tension between her and some of the other anchors, and also with some of the producers. Nevertheless, Crier has a first-rate, agile mind and is in touch with the issues. As the war ended, she got a wonderful opportunity to have her own show, Crier and Company, where she addresses vital issues with panelists, largely women.

Finally there is Bob Cain. Cain, who is a bit older than many of the anchors, has a maturity, a sense of timing, and a commitment to fairness that is quite impressive. He feels strongly about keeping a story on track and about taking action when he thinks the public is being misinformed or is not being given a full and balanced analysis. Let me cite a specific example. On the seventh day of the war, I was badly misquoted by a British officer, a group captain in Saudi Arabia, who felt I had criticized the RAF on CNN. Cain suggested to the producers that CNN run the group captain's criticism of me and immediately afterward let me comment on this criticism.

This process allowed me to say that I fully agreed with the group captain that it would be most inappropriate for a retired general in Atlanta with no first-hand knowledge to criticize the combat performance of the Royal Air Force. It also permitted me to point out that the group captain not only had my name wrong (he called me General Perry), but also had misunderstood what I had said about the loss of RAF aircraft. A few minutes later, the recently retired deputy prime minister of the United Kingdom, Sir Geoffrey Howe, in a live interview from the UK, praised the fact that I had been so complimentary about the Royal Air Force. So Cain was very helpful in encouraging the producers and me to recognize that there was a problem and in coming up with an idea for setting the record straight.

The real heart and soul of CNN is not the anchors but the producers. These men and women, almost never seen on camera, are responsible for planning and executing the daily schedule. They have the heavy responsibility of making sure that programs are balanced, interesting, dynamic, and responsive to fast-breaking news. These producers are talented and, in some cases, truly gifted. Probably the most dynamic, well known, controversial, and intense is Bob Furnad. He is a CNN senior vice president, but he steps in and serves, at times, as a supervising producer. He is responsible for live production throughout the entire day. Of course, he has some supervising producers working for him.

Supervising producers provide overall direction to the next two kinds of producers—executive producers and line producers. Although supervising producers are normally not in the pit, during the war they often moved there to provide minute-by-minute supervision of news production.

On the next level are executive producers, who are responsible for three-hour segments. Executive producers, in turn, oversee line producers who are responsible for one-hour segments. During the war, executive vice president Paul Amos handled the night shift and Furnad the day shift.

A producer whom I found to be particularly talented was Executive Producer Sue Bunda. She was responsible for a three-hour block each day. Bunda, who was pregnant (two months from having her baby when the war ended), had the kind of quiet competence that caused people to want to work with and for her. She was a rock-steady person at the helm during the key hours of the late morning.

A number of CNN reporters became familiar faces to the TV audience around the world as a result of the coverage and, even more important, the enormous amount of time people were spending watching CNN day after day. One individual who received a great many letters of praise was Charles Jaco, who reported from Saudi Arabia. There was some dramatic footage when there was a Scud attack and Jaco had to grab his gas mask. At that moment, the viewers got a feeling for the vulnerability of the reporter in the combat theater.

Jaco was often on camera to provide an analysis of the briefings that were given in Saudi Arabia, as well as to provide the flavor of combat. Jaco, a man who was not well known prior to the war, has now become an international celebrity. Perhaps this is because of his delivery, the excellence of his reporting, and the fact that he is an attractive and "tuned in" individual who was willing to take risks and continue reporting when Scuds were inbound to Saudi Arabia or, later, when explosions were occurring in Kuwait City.

Another reporter who came to the fore was Wolf Blitzer. Because his name is so unusual, and because he was reporting from the Pentagon, Wolf Blitzer became both a household name and a name for many comedy routines. He is not a defense expert, and initially he made a few mistakes. But he was a quick learner. He seemed to establish good contacts within the Pentagon, and toward the latter part of the war, he was very much on track as to what was going on within the military establishment and within the Pentagon. I challenged him on a couple of occasions on his interpretations of events. In one case I was right, and in another I was wrong. For instance, I made a mistake by saying, on camera, when Haifa

was attacked by a Scud missile, that it was the first. Within
seconds Blitzer corrected me. I appreciated his willingness to
challenge me and set the record straight. Blitzer, a man of
print journalism, having previously worked as the Washington correspondent for the *Jerusalem Post*, quickly became
an important part of the television scene.

John Holliman was reporting from Baghdad when the war
started along with Bernie Shaw and Peter Arnett. He, too,
became a household name because of his service there. Later
he reported from the Pentagon, along with Blitzer and Gene
Randall. The fact that Holliman was a man from a small town
in Georgia and had a kind of down-home, folksy approach to
the news made him very attractive to the television audience.
Holliman is a forthright fellow in whose analysis viewers
seem to put great faith and trust. He was very willing to admit
that he didn't have great journalistic experience in Baghdad,
in dealing with combat, or in addressing Pentagon issues.
This willingness to identify and acknowledge his weak areas
was, I think, appreciated by the audience; it made him an
excellent reporter because he asked the kinds of questions
that ordinary citizens would have asked.

One of the great success stories was the performance of
Christiane Amanpour. Her story is quite a remarkable one.
She started at the very lowest levels in CNN and worked her
way up to full-fledged reporter. Very bright and well traveled,
she pushes herself hard. She comes from Iranian parentage,
was born in London and has spent most of her life in Europe.
She has an intensity on the air that is very captivating. She
also has a hard edge to her questions. For instance, when she
was talking about what was happening in Baghdad and Iraq,
and when she was quoting the Iraqi government, she would
often use the phrase "the Iraqi government claims," whereas
Peter Arnett would have a tendency to say, "the Iraqi government said."

One of the more interesting aspects of Armanpour's impact
on CNN coverage out of Baghdad was that, once she was sent
there as the second reporter backing up Peter Arnett, Arnett
himself became a better correspondent. There was now
competition; she was asking more difficult questions of the
Iraqi government and pushing harder against the boundaries

of Iraqi censorship than Arnett had done when he was alone in Baghdad. She was also openly more skeptical of what the Iraqis were telling her. As a result Arnett himself asked tougher questions and was more critical of what he was hearing.

So as a result of Armanpour's arrival, the CNN coverage of the Baghdad and Iraqi story was improved. Interestingly enough, this was reflected in letters, faxes, and phone calls, which became less critical of CNN coverage out of Baghdad. Of course, Amanpour herself got a lot of very favorable mail for the way she was covering an important story.

Tom Johnson, President of CNN

The story of CNN and the war revolves around Tom Johnson and his willingness to empower CNN's executive vice president, Ed Turner. Tom Johnson's background is intriguing. He came from a poor family in Macon, Georgia, with a father who was never regularly employed and a mother who had to carry the burden for the family economically. When Johnson was fourteen, he landed a job as a copyboy at the local newspaper, the *Macon Telegraph*, and impressed its publisher, Leyton Anderson. Anderson paid Johnson's way to the University of Georgia and Harvard Business School.

Through his good fortune, the happy circumstance of getting to know powerful people who were willing to act as mentors, and his own talent and energy, Johnson moved from lower-middle-class circumstances in central Georgia to the

University of Georgia, Harvard University, a White House fellowship, and then to, while still a very young man, the key job of special assistant to President Johnson. He was still in his twenties when he worked directly for the President. Initially his mentor at the White House was Bill Moyers, but later Lyndon Johnson took a strong liking to this young Southerner.

When Lyndon Johnson left the White House in 1969, Tom Johnson, who was not related to the President, followed him to Texas to run the television station owned by the Johnson family. The Times Mirror's kingpin, Otis Chandler, discovered Tom Johnson and named him editor and later publisher of the *Dallas Times Herald*. Later Chandler moved him to California, where Johnson became the publisher of the *Los Angeles Times*. Johnson was in his early thirties when he got this big job. At a young age, he was able to impress older individuals, demonstrate his enormous potential for growth and leadership, and take advantage of the opportunities that were offered to him by such prominent mentors as Lyndon Johnson, Bill Moyers, and Otis Chandler.

Johnson's tenure as publisher of the *Los Angeles Times* was marked by a series of successes as that newspaper became the largest city newspaper in the country. But the year before Ted Turner made Johnson the offer to come to Atlanta, Otis Chandler retired as the chairman of Times Mirror. Shortly thereafter, the popular Tom Johnson was moved up to vice chairman of the Times Mirror Company and a new, more aggressive team was put in place at the *Los Angeles Times*. Although Johnson had been successful as the publisher of the *Times*, the suburban Orange County paper, the *Register*, was gaining readership at the expense of the *Los Angeles Times*, and for the first time since he was a teenager, Johnson had no mentor. Johnson suffered terrible withdrawal pains after being kicked upstairs. The position of vice chairman of the Times Mirror Company was not as exciting or as rewarding as that of publisher of one of the world's greatest newspapers.

Hence, Johnson was pleased to receive the offer of the CNN presidency from Ted Turner. Turner wanted to bring somebody to Atlanta to be the new president of CNN who could return unity and warmth to the CNN family. On his last day at the *Times*, Johnson wandered into the cafeteria and received a standing ovation that was so sustained and so warm it brought him to tears.

Meanwhile, back in Atlanta, CNN was in turmoil. It was time for Burt Reinhardt, who was in his late sixties, to step down as president. In 1989, Ted Turner had publicly announced that he would pick the new president from within CNN. There were three individuals who were hot competitors for the job. Ed Turner, a CNN executive from day one, had wide support among CNN staff members. Paul Amos, a "young Turk" who had built up Headline News to be a very effective organization, had the eye of Ted Turner as a real "comer." A third contender was Lou Dobbs, well known for his success in promoting economic reporting on CNN. Dobbs seemed to feel that he had an inside track for the position. This internal competition went on for almost a year, and there was lots of blood spilt in the battle.

Then, with little notice or warning, Ted Turner did what he had said he would not do. He reached outside the company and selected Tom Johnson. In the meantime, many people had lined up in general support of one of the three internal candidates. Ted Turner's selection of an outsider caused disappointment on the part of each of the three contenders and their respective allies.

The contender who seemed to take the decision best was Ed Turner. He went right back to work, getting out the news and continuing in his key role of executive vice president. Ed Turner soon established a close relationship with the new president. The other candidates did not accept the decision as magnanimously, so the late summer and fall of 1990 was a delicate period for Tom Johnson. In a remarkable coincidence, Tom Johnson came on board as the new president the day before Saddam Hussein invaded Kuwait. As a result, he received a rapid baptism of fire.

As someone who teaches leadership in many settings, I have often pointed out that a marvelous time to take over as a new chief executive, president, or boss is just when the activity level has picked up and everybody is especially intent on getting the job done. The new leader can get involved quickly, and the learning process can go much faster than in normal times. If the new boss does well in the next few months, he or she can soon be established as the legitimate leader.

Johnson was fortunate because he was able to learn quickly, to lend his support to ongoing plans, and to play the role of a "servant leader," that is, to support people in their needs and not get in their way or waste their time. Johnson wisely avoided giving many directions during those first few months. His attitude seemed to be one of "How can I help you?" or "What can I do to make your job easier?" Tom Johnson was very supportive of Ed Turner's initiatives. During the Gulf War, there seemed to be little tension between them.

Ed Turner is a man who is interested in getting the news out. If it bothered him that he had not been chosen to be the "big boss," he didn't publicly reveal his disappointment. In many ways, the job that Ed Turner has held in recent years as executive vice president is more attractive than the position of president, who tends to get mired down in the bureaucracy and has to spend a lot of time at corporate meetings. Ed Turner's job is basically one of chief operating officer. It is probably the best job for someone interested in being a newsman and staying close to what is happening within the network.

During the war Johnson had to make some tough decisions while, at the same time, taking heat from many sources. He had to decide whether to leave the team of Bernie Shaw, John Holliman, and Peter Arnett in Baghdad during the crucial period before the war began. He had to weigh the risks and decide whether it was, in fact, prudent to have CNN itself remain in the capital of the enemy. He also spent money lavishly to ensure that an airplane was available to get people out of Baghdad quickly, if that became necessary.

Tom Johnson possesses great self-confidence. How else can one explain his leaving the cushy life of the vice chairman of the Times Mirror Company and taking a job working for Ted Turner without a contract? Can he lead CNN from what is already the number one news network in the world to something even more important? Will he be able to hold a significant part of the Gulf War audience in quiet times? Will rivals, such as the new twenty-four-hour cable news network,

Monitor, do what CNN has been doing better, in more depth, and more accurately than CNN has been doing it? Can Johnson permit some of his most effective people to be lured away by bigger salaries to the other networks and still maintain and enhance CNN's level of excellence? Will he be able to keep Atlanta as the center of the news operation, or will there be more and more pressure to move toward the Washington news bureau, where so many networks and so much of the world is focused? Will he be able to keep the proper balance between domestic and international coverage?

Many of these are open questions, and only time will provide the answers. My own opinion of Johnson, after watching him very closely for six weeks, is that he is the man for the job. He has the maturity, good judgment, personality, and nurturing approach that should serve him well in this high-pressure medium.

```
┌──────────┐
│   ┌─┐    │
│   ╶┤└    │
│   └──┘   │
└──────────┘
```

How CNN Beat the
Competition

Although the news-gathering process, the roles that Tom
Johnson and Ed Turner played, and the vital role of the
producers have already been discussed, it may be useful to
look more carefully at all the elements that were vital in
ensuring the sustained success of CNN in presenting the
Gulf War and holding an enormous audience.

I cannot overemphasize the importance of the sorting
process. If a producer can choose from more than a dozen
stories coming into Atlanta, if that producer is empowered to
move to the best story without checking with any of his or her
bosses and if that producer is a savvy journalist who can
recognize the most important story, the result can be extraordinary journalism. I was frankly very impressed that the
CNN producers did not have to deal with a committee system

171

for decision making, that they were willing to make large decisions without checking with their bosses, and that they considered their jobs to be quite routine. Throughout the war, many of my contacts in the Pentagon and at the war colleges would tell me that they obtained better information quicker by watching CNN than from all the military intelligence and CIA sources combined. The reason CNN did better, in my judgment, was more extensive live hookups, better and quicker sorting, and faster decision making.

The other major American networks are designed to serve as entertainment networks and at the same time provide the viewer with the twenty-one-minute evening news and the two- or three-hour morning news shows. These networks do both of those jobs well. In the Gulf War, they did a fine job at expanding the half-hour evening news broadcast to an hour-long show. They also ran a great deal of special coverage. In fact, ABC, CBS, and NBC produced ten hours of war coverage per day, quite an impressive amount until a comparison is made with CNN. The three major networks were just not designed or manned to handle a multiplicity of fast-breaking news events and live coverage, especially in the hours between midnight and six AM.

A vital element of CNN's success was its firm commitment to taking the time and the trouble to provide balance in its news coverage. CNN executives and producers understood that every newsmaker wanted CNN to show him or her in a positive light. To put it more bluntly, it was the belief of the senior CNN producers that everyone who was not a CNN employee tried to "use" CNN. Although CNN executives were willing to accept material coming from many sources, they did it with a full understanding that some of the comments might be slanted, biased, or unbalanced. CNN thus worked hard to ensure that it had a multiplicity of news sources so that the viewer, over time, would obtain a broad perspective rather than getting a consistent "slant" from any particular direction.

The executives at CNN clearly understood that the reports from Baghdad were particularly susceptible to censorship and did, at times, reflect Iraq's propaganda. But my point is worth reemphasizing. CNN felt that everybody generating news, whether it was a Coalition military briefer or Saddam Hussein, attempted to put a positive spin on his message. Whether this spin was conscious or unconscious, CNN assumed that it was there.

It cannot be emphasized too much that CNN is a network for "news junkies." CNN covers only the news. CNN is not into soap operas, miniseries, game shows, movies, comedy, and live sports coverage. CNN does news, news, news. That is the primary reason employees are attracted to CNN. That is what drives and motivates people within CNN.

The mind-set of the news organizations at the other major networks is different. These networks tape most news segments and then splice them in such a way as to pack the maximum amount of news into the shortest possible time. This allows them to maximize the impact of every second of time they have. The approach requires a careful orchestration of material. But when asked to present a great deal of live material, to have a twenty-four-hour-a-day perspective, to present the news quickly from wherever it comes, these three networks just cannot perform like CNN. In fact, by the third day of the war, the three major networks were "back to the soaps."

Nevertheless, the three networks have some real advantages over CNN. Until quite recently, they have been well funded. They can present a story, in a short time, with considerable skill and clarity, and with excellent graphics and animation backup. This is very helpful to the viewer who is trying to understand what's going on and doesn't have much time to watch television. However, in the event of a major crisis or war, the viewer becomes willing to devote many hours throughout the day and night to following the crisis. The viewer who wishes to watch more than twelve hours a day only has three choices, CNN, CNN Headline News, and, to a lesser degree, C-Span.

A mythology has developed concerning CNN and its coverage of the Gulf War. Many people believe that CNN covered the war live. In small part that is true, but in a larger perspective it is not. As far as covering the war live is concerned, there were only a few instances of live combat coverage. For instance, the TV coverage out of Baghdad showing the antiaircraft fire was, on occasion, live (after CNN's portable satellite transmitter was installed in Baghdad on January 29, thirteen days after the war started, which permitted a direct satellite up-link from Baghdad).

With one exception, however, the viewers saw no Scuds coming inbound live. What the viewers saw of the Scuds appeared on tape. To many the coverage *seemed* live, since the television tape came into Atlanta only a very few minutes after the Scud had impacted the ground or been shot down by a Patriot missile. Viewers did see live, however, the fear in the faces of reporters in Saudi Arabia and Israel, and later in Kuwait and Iraq. Initially, the fear related to inbound Scud missiles and where they might land. Later, the fear related to uncertainties about the location of Iraqi combat units, mines, enemy troops, and unexploded ordnance. So, from that perspective, the viewers did get a bit of a feeling of what it was like to be in a combat zone.

It should be emphasized that the combat tape usually arrived within a few hours after the battle or the attack, a much faster process than during the war in Vietnam. The tapes came via satellite, so many people may have thought that they were seeing the war live, but that belief was largely erroneous.

Another interesting aspect involved the live coverage, again largely by CNN, of the briefings and news conferences. Viewers quickly realized they were not observing the highly structured presidential news conferences they had watched through the years. For the first time, the television audience saw the give and take, the dumb or aggressive questions, and the repetitive questioning used in the hope that more information on a critical issue might be elicited from the briefer.

During these briefings and news conferences, the viewers also observed the techniques the press used to try to break through the barriers of what the briefer attempted to withhold. This aggressive approach angered a large section of the viewing audience, who judged the press as arrogant, discourteous, and, at times, unpatriotic.

Another secret to CNN's exceptional performance was its ingeniuty in getting reliable coverage out of Baghdad. Before the war broke out, Eason Jordan, vice president for international affairs, wrote more than one hundred letters to various government officials in the Iraqi foreign ministry, information ministry, and television network, as well as to the Iraqi ambassador in Washington, asking for permission to broadcast live from Baghdad. Initially he failed to achieve success with his letters and telegrams.

Finally, a few days before the war commenced, Jordan obtained permission from the Iraqi government along the following lines: If the Iraqi television network could not provide the kind of service that CNN needed, CNN could use a portable transmitter (called a flyaway kit because it can be broken down into boxes that will fit into a commercial airliner) with a direct satellite up-link. With that as a basis, CNN decided to obtain the portable transmitter and get it ready for the trip to Baghdad. It was positioned in Amman just before war broke out. In fact, the plan was for CNN to drive it by truck from Amman to Baghdad on January 17, not exactly a flyaway solution, but effective nonetheless. Jordan wasn't worried, since he felt war would not commence immediately after the January 15 deadline.

When war began suddenly, CNN was stymied again. Jordan had to confirm with the Iraqi government that, in light of the radically changed circumstances, CNN still had permission to drive the television transmitter into Baghdad. Getting this reconfirmation took a while, so no live coverage came out of Baghdad for the first twelve days of the war. When CNN finally obtained permission from the Iraqi government, there was elation at CNN. The transmitter was driven over the hazardous road from Amman into Baghdad. At last, CNN had live television coverage from the enemy's capital.

These stubborn efforts to get television coverage out of Iraq led to a major breakthrough. For the first time in a war, there was live television emanating from a nation's capital that was under frequent air attack. Although most of the attacks came at night, there were a few occasions when military targets in and around Baghdad were hit by Tomahawk cruise missiles during the daytime. CNN obtained television coverage out of Baghdad before any other American network; consequently much of the American audience who might have been tempted to watch another network decided to stay with CNN.

Eason Jordan and his understanding of technical matters relating to both radio and television coverage, along with his solid persistence in working on the Iraqi government to get permission for CNN to use this equipment, became an important part of this success story.

Another problem to be solved in an always changing situation was knowing ahead of time which satellites would be needed and for how long. On an instant's notice, Dick Tauber, satellite and circuit manager, had to ensure that the satellites would be available so that, if a news story broke in Tel Aviv, the producers in Atlanta could switch quickly from Dhahran, Amman, Riyadh, or Jerusalem and back again. He came up with the idea of a twenty-four-hour system, which, at the push of a button, allowed CNN to switch around to many locations in the Middle East whenever there was news to report. I think it was generally acknowledged that the best coverage out of those key sites was provided by CNN. Handling the satellite paths so that the story would arrive in the Atlanta studio quickly was the key. Tauber did what many considered to be impossible, working out a system in advance, then making his system work under pressure.

Other stars of the CNN success story were Ken Jouts, Jim Miller, and Terry Frieden. They were producers in Saudi Arabia who worked closely with the Saudi government to try to maximize coverage from this important nation. The Saudi government was upset with CNN many times during the war, since CNN was the only television network that the Saudi government could receive from the United States. Whatever they did not like about American television, they saw on CNN, so working with the Saudis proved a delicate matter for these producers. CNN had to do its job while seeking to ensure that the Saudis didn't halt all reports out of Saudi Arabia. For instance, the Saudis were upset by CNN's coverage of the intercepts of the Scuds.

The Israeli government exhibited many of the same concerns. There were two twenty-four-hour-a-day Israeli censorship teams in Israel, one in the Jerusalem bureau of CNN and another in Tel Aviv. The situation became complicated because the Israeli censors would disagree with one another on what could be reported. So CNN had to negotiate not only with specific government officials from a particular bu-reaucracy but also with two different censors having different points of view on how to handle the news. The Israeli government was very concerned that Iraq might be using CNN coverage in Israel to better target future Scud attacks. This delicate multidimensional negotiation continued throughout the war.

Another area where CNN provided broader coverage than the other networks was in obtaining viewer reaction from the heartland of the United States. Earl Casey and his team of domestic producers and reporters were responsible for setting up hundreds of interviews around the country at military bases and nursing homes, and in small towns, medium-sized cities, and suburbs to get the reaction of the person on the street about the coverage of the war. Generally, there was strong public support for the war, and these reports seemed to reinforce among the American viewing audience its general support of the Bush administration. Although this CNN grass-roots coverage was not intended to engender support for the U.S. government, it turned out that way. More important, the comments of so many Americans demonstrated to viewers around the globe that there was strong public support in the United States for President Bush and his leadership. These viewers also got a good idea through CNN of the various reasons for this support.

Because some reporters spent so much time on the air, several producers had to play many of the roles of reporters. For instance, Wolf Blitzer at the Pentagon spent so much time standing by to be on camera when called upon by the senior producer in Atlanta or Washington that he was not able to spend much time digging for news. This situation put a heavy burden on Sol Levine, the CNN producer in the Pentagon. He had to play many roles, including technician, researcher, reporter's assistant, and telephone answerer. This general pattern was true for producers in many different locations in the United States and overseas. They were doing double duty because so many of the reporters were "captured by the camera."

To gain and hold a television audience, a network has to demonstrate objectivity. One way that CNN tried to do this was to show letters on camera that had come into the CNN studios over the course of the previous day or two. Many of these letters were very critical of CNN and the CNN coverage of the Gulf War. The use of these letters on camera showed to the viewers that CNN officials were reading these letters and were willing to share criticism with the viewers. Let me highlight a couple of those. The first one appeared on camera during the first week of the war, the second just after Arnett interviewed Saddam Hussein.

> We Americans *do not* want more and more details and not any that can help the enemy. It is not your "job" to keep Americans and the world informed. You have a greater responsibility to protect the national and world interest by restraint. I also feel that you give too much time to those who march in the streets, burn flags, and block buildings to show opposition to the war and to the President.

> When Saddam Hussein called the President of the United States of America a liar and Peter Arnett did not flinch; when Saddam Hussein claimed that Israel had bombarded Iraq and Peter Arnett never followed that statement with a single question designed to expose his source of knowledge; and when Saddam Hussein spoke of his 'peaceful' ways without a single return question from Arnett with respect to the Iraqi invasion of Kuwait or the abuse of POWs—it became apparent to me that he and CNN had simply sold out. Shame on both of you.

Every day there were a few letters that were shown on the screen and read by the anchors at the same time. Selecting those letters proved an interesting exercise. They were screened by Zola Murdock's staff, which read each of the incoming letters. Anybody who saw a letter that might be interesting to the viewers, and particularly one that was quite critical, would bring it to the attention of a supervising producer or to vice president Bob Furnad, who would then make the final selection for use on the air. I entered the process a few times when I found a letter that I felt was especially interesting, and I would hand it to Bob Furnad. He used my suggestions on a couple of occasions. During this whole process, I never saw any attempt by CNN to not use a letter on camera that was very critical, although CNN did screen out profanity. CNN executives seemed anxious to put both praise and criticism on camera. This is another example of CNN's searching very hard for balance throughout the entire war.

There were many polls taken during the war asking the public which network provided the best war coverage. Most such polls accorded CNN the highest marks. For instance, a Times Mirror poll showed 61 percent chose CNN as the best, 12 percent chose ABC, and 7 percent each CBS and NBC (PBS, Fox, C-Span and others shared the remaining 13 percent). The 61 percent amounts to more Americans than have cable TV. Clearly many people who did not have CNN in their homes found ways to watch CNN elsewhere: on the job, in bars, at hotels, in airports, and on the local affiliates of ABC, CBS, and NBC when they used the CNN feed to keep viewers abreast of the war.

If information is power and if information via television is both money and power, then CNN's future is bright if it can hold even a small portion of the huge audience it attracted during the war. In April 1991, CNN's audience was 17 percent higher than it was in April 1990. This is the kind of ratchet-up effect that CNN's coverage of each major crisis seems to have on viewers. Ted Turner created the new model for television news coverage. Tom Johnson, Ed Turner, Eason Jordan, Bob Furnad, Gail Evans, and many others have implemented it and refined it.

Ted Turner's role during the war may be of interest. He stayed very much in the background during the Gulf War. He was quietly supportive of Tom Johnson and Ed Turner when costs were way up and revenues were down during Desert Shield and Desert Storm. He was seldom seen in the CNN headquarters in Atlanta during the war, and when he did drop by, it was to thank employees and not to micromanage the network. I saw him only once—in the cafeteria. He shook my hand, told me I was doing a good job, and was gone in less than a minute. I never saw Jane Fonda.

26

The Gulf War and Freedom of the Press

In the aftermath of the Gulf War a raging debate has gone on within the media and in the schools of journalism. It focuses on the issue of freedom of the press, censorship, manipulation of the media by the Pentagon and the White House, and the profound implications this manipulation has for the future. This concern was expressed by Peter Jennings in a graduation speech he delivered at Gallaudet University on May 10. As the May 20, 1991, issue of *USA Today* reported exerpts from this speech: "There are Americans who believed during this war that the American press should have quietly abided by all military restrictions in the name of national security. You know as well as I do that in this war, unlike any other in the nation's history, the US military mounted a major effort to suffocate impartial reporting. The military establishment was apparently so fearful that the press would have an objective view of its behavior that thousands of man-hours, at taxpayers' expense, were spent trying to keep the American press corps in quarantine.... Do we really want a military establishment in the United States which hides from the cameras?... I think it's rather sad there was no opportunity for millions of us to see anything of the bravery or dedication of the US soldiers on the battlefield."

Of course, the press in part became frustrated because the American viewers didn't seem very concerned about censorship of the media by Defense Secretary Cheney or General Schwarzkopf. The press could and did criticize Saddam Hussein, who ordered some very inhumane acts, including murdering his own citizens, taking over a defenseless country, killing and raping large numbers of Kuwaiti citizens, releasing millions of gallons of oil into the Persian Gulf, and setting off oil well and refinery fires in Kuwait. But during the war itself, when it came to criticizing the United Nations, members of the Coalition, the President of the United States, the military and its conduct of the war, the press hadn't much critical meat to chew on.

Judy Milestone, a very savvy person in the CNN booking office, made these points when I asked her why there seemed to be so little criticism of the President and the military during the Gulf War. Milestone indicated that, when the government seems to have its act together and when there is strong support throughout the nation for the activities of the President and the military, most members of the press are not inclined to criticize heavily.

However, some members of the media feel that if they are not constantly criticizing our institutions, our national leaders, and our military commanders, our democratic system will deteriorate over time. This is the "slippery slope" argument: Give national leaders a respite from criticism and they will destroy our democratic institutions with their power and their arrogance.

Should one report favorably when an institution performs well and meets its goals, whether it is the Roman Catholic Church, the New York Stock Exchange, the Department of the Treasury, or the United States Marine Corps? Does praise, in fact, undermine freedom of the press? I feel quite strongly that a critical press plays a very important role in this country and is absolutely vital for the working of our democracy. There's no question that some people in powerful positions in and out of government have a tendency to abuse that power; the press can be very useful in highlighting that abuse. On the other hand, I am not at all sure that some praise, particularly over a short period of time, say six weeks, and the withholding of information for a few days in order to save lives undermine the constitutional principle of freedom of the press.

There's another dimension to the issue of the press coverage of the Gulf War. Columnists like Anthony Lewis raised the point that the United States press during the Gulf War pandered to the conservative and patriotic proclivities of the American public and did not, in fact, do its job. Lewis raises an important question. If the public which reads newspapers and magazines and watches television and listens to the radio is profoundly biased in some way, and if the press, in turn, plays to that bias in order to gain or maintain readership or viewership, are we not, in fact, in danger of giving away one of the most sacred and important powers of the democratic system?

Lewis H. Lapham, in a very angry article in the May issue of *Harper's Magazine*, titled "Trained Seals and Sitting Ducks," is even more critical than Lewis of the press in this regard. This debate will continue for many years in the aftermath of this war and needs to be seriously engaged by people on all sides on the issue. It is my belief that institutions do, in fact, need to be looked at very critically on a continuing basis. John Sununu's flying around in a government airplane (with stewards aboard to take care of his every whim) to visit his dentist and to hit the ski slopes is just the kind of arrogance of power that the press can and should highlight in order to rein in someone who seems to have forgotten that a public office is a public trust.

But should an institution that has been so vilified for so many years as has the United States military be praised when it performs well? One can argue that it is in the public interest, and even in the constitutional interest, that institutions be given some praise for operating effectively, efficiently, and compassionately. Perhaps the admiration of Norman Schwarzkopf, Dick Cheney, and Colin Powell is overplayed. At the same time it strikes me as healthy when we find some heroes who can serve as role models.

I'm a great believer that this country, particularly its young people, need role models. For instance, I am writing a book about Lt. Col. Jimmy Dyess, of Augusta, Georgia, who earned the Carnegie Medal for saving two lives at great risk to his own when he was eighteen years old. Later he earned, posthumously, the nation's highest award for combat heroism, the Medal of Honor, as a battalion commander in the US Marine Corps. Dyess is the only person in history to have earned our nation's top peacetime and wartime awards for heroism.

I don't think it's inappropriate that a man of such enormous humanity and self-sacrifice should be praised in the newspapers and in magazines. It is not, it seems to me, undermining the great power of the press to find role models and focus attention on them when they perform outstanding service or at some later time when their contributions to their nation and to mankind are fully understood.

I think members of the press (both print and electronic) should be careful not to assume that the only role they have to play is constant criticism. The press as an institution is not well regarded in this country. It ranks quite low compared to other institutions, such as the church, the medical profession, the military, the teaching profession, and others in public service. If the only role that the press were to play was constant criticism, it could slide down a self-initiated slippery slope of cynicism, which will not serve the people or our constitutional system well. However, my personal experience during the Gulf War at CNN, with many radio stations and with most newspaper and magazine reporters, reconfirms in my mind that there is a healthy skepticism, but little cynicism, about what government officials are doing and saying.

27

CNN Faces the Future

As a teacher of leadership, I welcome the opportunity to observe at close hand large organizations at work. My CNN experience was an extremely rich and rewarding one. Because I had a unique opportunity to work for CNN for a short, intense period of time, and could observe the leadership team and the staff function in a high-pressure setting, I learned quite a bit about their strengths and weaknesses. I have covered many of CNN's strengths. Let me now hit its errors and weaknesses.

CNN made many errors during the Gulf War. Let me list a few. CNN was late getting the telestrators (the John Madden machines for highlighting strike camera film or movement of forces on maps). The two full-time military analysts should have had the telestrators available and received training on them before the war broke out. Another weak area for CNN was animation. CNN did not have a first-rate team of animators because it didn't spend the money to provide the people or the technology for first-rate animation and graphics. The result of this neglect was clear throughout the war. CNN did less well than the other networks in educating millions through the magic of animation. CNN did bring in an expert from California to work on animation, and he did a nice job, but he arrived after the war commenced, and it took him a while to get up to speed.

One problem CNN never solved related to the unreliability of interrupted feedback devices. These are the earpieces that allow producers to talk to an anchor, a reporter, or a guest who is on camera or about ready to go on camera. They are called interrupted feedback (IFB) devices because the wearer/ speaker cannot hear themselves over these devices when they talk—the feedback from the voice is permanently interrupted. At times at CNN, just when a producer needed to send an important message to an anchor, reporter, or guest, the message could not be heard through the earpiece. This problem continued throughout the war. On a number of occasions, I was asked to fill up camera time until some IFB problem was solved in Saudi Arabia, New York, Baghdad, or other locations.

Other areas of CNN's weaknesses related to the anchors. A few of the twenty CNN anchors performed poorly under the pressures of covering this war; they were basically readers and not journalists. They were unable to formulate the best questions as they reacted to an answer to a previous question. Also, they did not understand why a producer wanted to move to the next story. Hence, they failed to make transitions particularly well. When they made the transition, instead of explaining, "There is an important event going on in Tel Aviv. There's a new Scud attack, and we are going to break out of this briefing and take you live to Israel," they would say, "Now we are going to go to Tel Aviv." (Two anchors were quietly let go after the war as a result of these shortcomings.)

Hence, this war was a proving ground for many people. Some producers who did not make the best decisions were moved to less demanding positions.

The war at CNN could be compared to a war for the military. As a flight leader in combat over Vietnam, I could usually tell after a few missions if a newly arrived aviator could "hack it" in the tough combat environment. If he couldn't, we scheduled him for milk runs over easy targets and never checked him out as a flight leader. CNN executives made the same types of choices during this war.

For a network that prides itself in being truly international and which reaches, in times of major international crises and war, over a billion viewers in 108 nations, CNN has very few foreigners in its main studio in Atlanta. Yet if a network is going to provide international news, it should have among its employees a large proportion having an international perspective. Most Americans are not well traveled, and if you hire mostly Americans, you are likely to wind up with an American slant on the news. Ted Turner's stated purpose of having a real international network is being subverted, in part, by the use, among his news gatherers, of Americans who have not spent much time outside the United States. If CNN is going to be the great international network of the future, it has to be much more aggressive in hiring Americans with many years of experience living and working in other countries, and even more necessary, in employing people from other countries and bringing them to Atlanta to work.

A key question following the postwar euphoria is how well CNN will deal with success. Will it become complacent? Will it become arrogant? Will it become bureaucratic? Will the demands of employees for higher pay cause a negative cash flow? I think the chances are excellent that success will not go to the heads of CNN executives and its other employees. First of all, solid leadership is in place. The CNN executives understand who they are and where they are going. They are not likely to be carried away with the success they achieved in covering this war. In addition, with the other networks continuing to lay off personnel, the pressure to raise salaries at CNN should not be severe. It's unlikely that CNN will decide to hire two-million-dollar anchors with their tendency toward power trips, arrogance, aloofness, and "image polishing." Hence, CNN should remain, for the foreseeable future, both profitable and successful.

CNN will also continue to attract the vital talent needed for television news gathering, news production, and news reporting. TV journalists want opportunities to make contributions. If they are reporters or anchors, they want to be on camera. Journalists are happy if they have a chance to produce, if they can see their work leading to something (most important, being used on the air) and not ending up on the cutting room floor. One thing that twenty-four-hour television has plenty of is "air time."

Another important part of twenty-four-hour television news is the many opportunities for live television. The beauty of appearing live is that what you do and say is what people see. No editorial presence intervenes. In the immediate post-Gulf War era, more people have applied for work at CNN than ever before, despite the low pay scales. According to Ed Turner, he is receiving five hundred unsolicited self-promotional television tapes a month from job applicants. The opportunity to pick and choose among an enormous number of talented applicants will be CNN's blessing for many years to come. Hence, if CNN executives are careful in the selection process, the quality of its personnel should gradually improve.

Although they are genuinely warm and caring people, CNN executives understand that, on occasion, they have to fire people: the producers who do not respond quickly and cannot operate well under pressure, the anchors who are attractive readers rather than savvy journalists, and research and staff writers who can't collect data rapidly and write well. The contracts for anchors enable CNN to release them from employment in rather short order. A three-year contract is quite common, but a "revisit" every thirteen weeks or six months is also the norm. In other words, it is quite easy to discontinue an anchor who can't seem to get to work on time or who performs poorly in normal times or in times of stress. In fact, an anchor was fired shortly after the war ended for a rather basic reason—getting to work late too often.

It is likely that CNN will remain a meritocracy in which ideas are king and queen. If you produce, you will be rewarded; if you don't, you won't. Hence, CNN should be able to avoid the problems of postwar complacency and arrogance and should continue to innovate and push the boundaries of technology to provide even better live coverage of fast-breaking events.

For those who might be interested in learning more about the issues of television journalism, I would like to commend the recent book by Robert and Gerald Jay Goldberg, *Anchors: Brokaw, Jennings, Rather and the Evening News* (Birch Lane Press, 1990). The contrast between how CNN and the three major networks in the United States produce the news is stark. CNN's success in covering the Gulf War is largely a result of its planning, persistence, technical skills, and leadership. However, the fact that CNN takes a team approach with everyone helping to get the best story on camera throughout the day and the night contributed to this success. Something was lost when the anchors on the three major networks gained so much power in the late 1970s.

It will be interesting to watch if, when, and how these networks adapt to tough competition from CNN. In the future the competition of the ABC, CBS, and NBC news bureaus may be more with CNN and less with one another. Many viewers have shared with me, as I travel around the country, their new approach to CNN. Since the war broke out, they switch on a TV set and choose CNN or CNN Headline News to find out what is going on. If all is quiet in the world, then and only then do they go to another network.

During the Gulf War, more than eighty news organizations from the United States and around the world visited the CNN headquarters. Japanese, British, French, Italian, Dutch, and Australian television networks came and took copious notes. Clearly CNN will face future competition from emerging twenty-four-hour cable news networks. For instance, Monitor, which is billing itself as the "thinking person's CNN," started its twenty-four-hour-a-day news coverage on the first of May 1991. Although it is available in only a few cities, Monitor has plans to expand steadily, taking advantage of fiber-optic technology that will allow the viewer the option of more than a hundred and fifty channels. In addition, I expect to see twenty-four-hour television news emanating from a number of other countries by the turn of the century.

A number of enterprises in and around major American cities are experimenting with round-the-clock local news. Viewers on Long Island, New York, and in Orange County,

California, already have this service available, and by the end of 1992, new cable channels will be on line in Chicago and Washington, D.C. The Orange County News Channel has already gone beyond strictly local news; it sent reporters to Saudi Arabia and Israel during the Gulf War.

If this kind of competition encourages CNN to provide more in-depth coverage of major issues, so much the better. Who knows, CNN may one day "dare to be boring" on some of its in-depth shows in order to reach a higher level of journalistic maturity.

Final Impressions

The end of my days at CNN came quickly. The day after the war was over, at mid-morning, Gail Evans, my de facto boss for six weeks, asked, "Are you ready to go home?" I said, "I sure am." She invited me to appear on camera one more time for some wrap-up comments, after which my task would be done. So the finish was crisp and to the point, just the way I wanted it. My commitment had been for the duration of the war, and the war was over. There was no reason for me to linger. Evans conducted a little ceremony in the booking office, where my newfound friends said some nice things about me and gave me some presents (a CNN baseball hat and a CNN T-shirt are my favorites). I thanked the folks in booking for all their assistance, then went down to the anchor desk for my last hurrah.

Let me close this account with some final impressions that

came out of this incredibly intense and interesting experience.

The scramble for camera time. It was fascinating to see how many people tried to fight their way in front of the cameras at CNN. Evans and her staff received, by the thousands, letters, phone calls, pleas, and inquiries—from military experts, political experts, economic experts, technical experts, and regional experts, all offering their services. These people wanted to be part of this story by appearing on television. Some people were quite miffed when they volunteered their services and were not asked to appear on camera. I often observed the bookers as they gently let someone know by telephone they would not be needed.

Some of the people who called to volunteer their services were big names. The call to CNN booking from a member of Oliver North's staff comes to mind. Throughout the war, the CNN booking staff was tough-minded, operating on the premise that what mattered was substance and objectivity. Those who were invited to appear on CNN generally did well and gave thoughtful answers to questions. A few were "tap dancers": they gave answers whether they knew anything or not. A few overstated their credentials and their knowledge in order to get a chance to appear on CNN. This perhaps helped them get a first invitation, but when they did poorly, they were not invited back. What was impressive to me was how well CNN screened the candidates for interviews. Very few tap dancers ever made it to the CNN anchor desks in Atlanta, Washington, or elsewhere.

The imperious anchor. As I talked to people who served as military analysts at the other networks, I found that there was present a factor, which I will label the imperious anchor, that diminished the ability of these military analysts to make a significant contribution. Some of the military analysts shared with me how difficult it was to get ideas in to the anchors in order to help these anchors frame the questions that would be most interesting and relevant. The military analysts were, at times, quite frustrated because they didn't think the questions from the anchors were particularly good. Also they weren't given enough time to answer the questions that did come.

Consequently, I have come to the conclusion that some military experts who were viewed as not being very thoughtful or very thorough in their analysis were unfairly criticized. They were capable of doing better, but were constrained either by time or the inability to get the best questions asked. It is *possible* to give a brilliant answer to a poorly posed question, but it is not *easy*, especially if you are given only a minute and a half to do so. This was not a problem for me, because I had direct access to the anchors and the opportunity to speak directly to the scriptwriters; I had to field very few questions that were way off the mark. Although I sometimes was not given enough time to answer questions fully, I got much more time than military analysts from the other networks.

The too-many-guests phenomenon. My favorite television news program, the MacNeil-Lehrer NewsHour on PBS, did a superb job of providing in-depth analysis on the most important issues of each twenty-four-hour period of the war. However, there was a tendency to assemble too many panelists. This need to "overbook" seems to grow out of the fear that, if too few panelists were brought in and one or two of them did not make useful contributions, the MacNeil-Lehrer NewsHour might be stuck with a segment with little substance. The MacNeil-Lehrer policy seemed to be, when in doubt, err on the side of numbers.

This approach leads to too few questions for each guest and not enough follow-up on interesting answers before time runs out. Other networks, including CNN, also suffered at times from too many panelists. Occasionally at CNN I was frustrated with the half-hour late-evening show, "Gulf Talk," when I found that Bernard Shaw was going to have four guests rather than two, as James Blackwell or I had suggested.

The tragic record of Robert McNamara. One of the saddest realizations to come out of this war was a heightened awareness among American citizens of how poorly the Vietnam War had been managed and led. We now have the opportunity to see that a war can be fought brilliantly through the empowerment of a field commander and the use of carefully developed strategies, doctrine, tactics, and surprise. The military success of the Gulf War caused me and many others to look back sorrowfully to Vietnam, where over 2 million Americans served and 58,000 gave their lives, including my best friend. It need not have been.

From the new perspective of the Gulf War experience, Secretary of Defense Robert McNamara appears a tragic figure indeed. McNamara tried to micromanage the war from the Pentagon, did not respect or trust most of the top military leaders. Also, McNamara never straightened out command arrangements to insure that there was a single theater commander and a single air component commander reporting directly to this theater commander.

Future defense secretaries would be wise to ask the Department of Defense historian for a careful comparison of the leadership styles and substance of Dick Cheney and Robert McNamara. I would hope that the Cheney model will prevail in the decades ahead. In addition, I hope we grasp the lessons of the Gulf War and reinforce the lessons of the Vietnam War.

Ethical issues. When I drove to Atlanta the night the war broke out, I expected that I would have to deal with some issues relating to ethics. The first came up on the seventh day of the war. I wanted to recommend three books to help viewers better understand this war. One of the books, *The Air Campaign*, is part of a series for which I am the general editor. I receive royalties on each book in this series. I didn't feel it would be ethical for me to recommend a book on television for which I was receiving compensation, however modest. I resolved this dilemma by writing the publisher that day and telling him to send all royalty checks from that day forward to my church in Augusta. The other ethical issue I have already discussed: my belief that some of the reports coming out of Baghdad were misleading.

Perhaps the most poignant moment in the war. This moment occurred when the TV pictures came through CNN and other networks showing four Iraqi soldiers surrendering to an American. The Iraqis kissed the American's hand and displayed great fear. The television viewers observed the compassion, care, and empathy on the part of that American fighting man as he reassured these downtrodden Iraqi soldiers that they were going to be all right. It was an important moment in the television coverage of this war, because it told a powerful story in just a few seconds. These soldiers who only moments before were locked in combat did not hate one another. The American soldiers and the soldiers of the Coalition were interested not in punishing the Iraqi soldiers, but only in ending the war as quickly, painlessly, and bloodlessly as possible.

Overblown concerns. Media attention was directed to a number of subjects for which I think the concern was largely overblown. For instance, there was a great deal of discussion about how children were going to be traumatized by watching this war on television. Certainly there was trauma on the part of some children, but viewing this war closely on CNN and the other networks may have been beneficial to many children.

Because I experienced the Japanese bombing of Pearl Harbor, I became aware at age six of some of the harsh realities of world politics. I remember carefully reading newspapers and magazines throughout World War II about the progress of the war, especially the Italian campaign, in which my father served. Conversations around our family breakfast table concerned Churchill's leadership, the role of America in the postwar world, alliance warfare, and the difficulties that Eisenhower faced. They were very much a part of my life as a young child. In retrospect, World War II gave me an intellectual motivation (from age six through age ten) that has served me well for almost fifty years.

The Gulf War has made youngsters around the world aware that our planet can be a dangerous place and that leaders in certain countries can be real monsters. On the other hand, they also have had a chance to observe leaders who may become role models for them. They may also have learned about the geography of the Middle East and the role of the United Nations. So the enhanced intellectual development of young people may be one result of this six weeks of war and its aftermath. Many young people may henceforth read newspapers more carefully, be more interested in world geography, world and military history, and take their courses in school more seriously. These benefits could be significant ones, especially for this country, which will continue to be the most strategically important nation in the world for at least the next two decades.

There was a raging debate before and during the war about

whether there was a disproportionate number of blacks involved in the war, with the consequent possibility that they might be killed or wounded in disproportionate numbers. The various networks devoted much airtime to discussing this issue. In the final analysis, the number of soldiers killed, both in combat and in accidents, was very low. A racial breakout of combat fatalities showed deaths in proportion to the normal distribution of racial populations. Altogether, 142 Caucasions, or 78 percent of the total were killed; 27 blacks, or 15 percent; 8 Hispanics, or 4 percent; and 1 Asian-American, or less than 1 percent. Six women were killed in combat; they constituted 3 percent of the total.

Blacks constituted 12.1 percent of the US population in the 1990 census, while Hispanics made up 9 percent, Asian-Americans 3 percent, and Native Americans less than 1 percent. While the female death toll represented 3 percent, women constituted 6 percent of the Desert Storm force and 11.5 percent of the active duty military overall. The number of women killed in combat was disproportionately low; but, of course, there are many legal and policy restrictions on women that limit their exposure to hostile fire. The total of 182 deaths includes those resulting from hostile fire and those from other causes such as friendly fire and aircraft crashes during the six-week Gulf War.

Unexpected pleasures. Throughout this war I was constantly being surprised by little things. One nice surprise was how much I was trusted by the executives of CNN. Let me cite a specific example. During the six weeks I worked for CNN, Ed Turner always listened to me very carefully. About the first of February, I told Ed that since I assumed he was a planner, he would be interested in knowing how long this war might last. I mentioned to him that it was clear to me that the war would be short and would probably end by the first of March. I emphasized that the war was progressing better than Schwarzkopf was reporting because he didn't want to "over-report," that is, to report things he was not sure he had accomplished. Hence, in my judgment, the "gloom and doom" analysts were way off the mark. I suggested that he might want to get CNN ready to cover the postwar stories, since Kuwait would soon be liberated.

Unbeknownst to me, Turner passed on my prediction

through the Basys computer system to his key people in Atlanta, Washington, and in the field and asked them to conduct their research and reporting with my prediction in mind. Turner also suggested to them that any official or "expert" who talked about a long war should be listened to with great skepticism. Just after Kuwait was liberated, Turner told me that my prediction had been very helpful to CNN and its coverage of the war, because everyone was able to look at its probable termination date realistically and with a focused view. The fact that he put faith in my prediction even to the point of spreading the word to many others in the network showed a level of trust that really touched me.

Unsung heroes. The brain trust in the Pentagon (the Checkmate team) that developed the plan for the air campaign and worked so hard behind the scenes to come up with new ideas, new analyses, and new insights to provide to the field tops my list of the unsung. The planning and operational staff in Saudi Arabia under the guidance of Lt. Gen. Charles Horner, the air component commander, deserves much credit for the implementation of the forty-two day air campaign. Gens. Buster Glosson, Patrick Caruana, and Larry Henry, and Lt. Cols. Dave Deptula and Sam Baptiste, Majs. Mark B. "Buck" Rogers and David Waterstreet, and Capt. William Brunner, as well as many others pulled together the most complex air campaign in history. The fact that over 110,000 combat sorties were flown with only one mid-air collision is absolutely amazing to me. Kudos also must go to the planners of the one-hundred-hour ground campaign.

Institutions which made a significant contribution to the planning and execution of this war but were seldom mentioned on the air were the five United States war colleges. These colleges educate the majority of the top American leaders in strategy and in the operational level of warfare. Let me give you a specific example. National War College graduates who played prominent parts in the war include the President's national security advisor, Brent Scowcroft; General Colin Powell; Nate Howell, the US Ambassador to Kuwait, who was confined to the embassy for so many months after Iraq invaded Kuwait; Lt. Gen. Frederick M. Franks Jr., US Army, commander of the US Seventh Corps; Brig. Gen.

Richard I. "Butch" Neal, US Marine Corps, the chief US briefer in Saudi Arabia; four air force wing commanders— John M. "Boomer" McBroom, the commander of the First Tactical Fighter Wing (F-15s); Alton C. "Al" Whitley Jr., commander of the Stealth fighter unit; Hal M. Hornberg, the commander of the F-15E wing; and Merrill R. "Ron" Karp, commander of the F-4G squadrons that attacked radar sites so effectively. Many of these leaders were students when I was commandant of the National War College. It was a pleasure observing them do so well as commanders and as articulate spokesmen. They appeared often on various television networks. Many graduates of the various war colleges used the strategic perspectives they had gained at these schools to plan and implement one of the most successful military campaigns in American history.

Much credit should go to those who were responsible for moving supplies, ensuring proper sanitation and medical care, providing gasoline and jet fuel in loading and fixing tanks, artillery pieces, armored personnel carriers, airplanes, and helicopters. I was especially impressed by the performance of the tanker crews of the air force, navy, and Marine Corps. Many reserve and National Guard units were called up and served with distinction during the Gulf War. The performance of the Air National Guard units which flew over 3,400 combat sorties over enemy territory was especially impressive.

Gen. Lew Allen, Jr., the chief of staff of the air force in the early 1980s, deserves recognition. He saw the wisdom of a robust strategic planning system, and he welcomed the long-range planners as they presented to him every month some radical ideas and concepts. The success of the air campaign, in part, is the result of Allen's visionary leadership. I would hope the present chief of staff, Gen. Merrill McPeak, who is in the process of building a new organizational structure for the air force, will reinstitute, fully support, and pass on to his successor a strategic planning system that once worked so well.

On the CNN side there were many unsung stars. The viewers of CNN during this war got to know the anchors and the reporters quite well. What they didn't see were the hundreds of staff people who worked at a feverish pace to help report this story. In a war or a crisis there is much work to be done as well as many areas of frustration. For instance, the script writers worked at high speed to support the anchors, yet much of their material was not used when fast-breaking events destroyed the normal schedule. Burt Reinhardt, who, as CNN's second president, put CNN on a solid financial footing, provided wise advice to the new president both prior to and during the Gulf War. He has served as vice chairman (there is no chairman) of CNN since early August 1990.

The most overused phrase. "The mother of all battles." That seems to be a kind of rough translation of what Saddam Hussein was saying. Now we have the the "mother of all" defeats, the "mother of all" oil shocks, the "mother of all" disasters, the "mother of all" this, and the "mother of all" that. Even George Bush is using the phrase, labeling Barbara "the Mother of all Bushes" at the forty-seventh annual dinner of radio and television correspondents.

Biggest disappointments. First, the uneven coverage of the war by the *New York Times*. Its political reporting by journalists like Thomas L. Friedman was first rate, but its coverage of military activities was unimpressive. Recent front-page coverage of the Kitty Kelly book on Nancy Reagan and the naming, and character assassination, of an alleged rape victim at the Kennedy estate in Palm Beach, Florida, may indicate that the poor military reporting during the war is just one example of the journalistic and ethical decline of the *Times*.

Second, the performance of some "military experts" was quite disappointing. In answer to specific questions, some analysts would guess or "wing it." As a result, they misled and confused viewers on occasion. Lt. Gen. Mick Trainor of ABC, who in my judgment did a fine job of answering questions by sticking to what he knew and not guessing or speculating, described one of the more prominent "military analysts" as "often wrong but never in doubt."

Third, the poor performance of the Air Force Association throughout the crisis and war. This association, which has the mission of supporting air power and serving its members, did little of either prior to and during the war. John Warden's great book, *The Air Campaign*, has been part of the Air Force

Association's discount-book program for two years; yet the association never publicized this program among its members. The result was that many association members who should have studied this seminal book prior to the war did not do so. In my judgment, there would have been much less resistance to the Checkmate plan for the air campaign by certain senior officers in the Pentagon, at Tactical Air Command and in Saudi Arabia had they obtained, read, and understood this book prior to August 2, 1990.

Fourth, the failures of intelligence, particularly in estimating the number of Scud launchers available to Saddam Hussein prior to the war.

Fifth, the unbalanced criticism by Sen. Alan Simpson of Peter Arnett. Certainly Arnett deserved criticism, but he was never a sympathizer of Saddam, and he provided some useful information to both viewers and Coalition officials.

Sixth, the lack of strategic planning within the American government for the postwar world. Before and during the Gulf War, there should have been an aggressive planning effort to examine various "alternative futures" for the postwar world. Even a superficial examination of historical experiences with war termination and the aftermath of war would have made clear to planners and decision makers that there might be chaos following this war. After World War II, the Korean War, and the Vietnam War, there were huge refugee and displaced person problems. Leaders with any kind of historical perspective should have anticipated and planned for such a contingency. Good postwar planning could have reduced significantly the agony and the death of so many Kurdish people. President Bush needs to hire some strategic planners quickly, or he will go down in history as an In-Box President who solves problems well but lacks that vital quality of a major leader, vision. Leadership is much more than maintaining a high rating in the polls, internetting well, and getting to the bottom of your in box.

How this experience has changed my life. I truly enjoyed my six weeks in the sun and greatly appreciate those who continue to come up to me and thank me for my efforts to help people understand the Gulf War. My phone rings much more often than before January 16, 1991, and I have received many more invitations to speak than I can possibly accept. Also, interest in my most recent books, *Taking Charge* and *Assignment Pentagon*, has so dramatically escalated that I have established a toll-free number for those who would like copies (1–800–448–4332). I no longer work for CNN and hope that I never have to narrate another war, but I have appeared on other programs, including all three Augusta network channels, South Carolina public television, and the Robert Schuller hour. By midsummer of 1991, my life had happily begun to return to normal. My next project is to complete a book on Jimmy Dyess of Augusta, the only person to have earned the Carnegie medal for peacetime heroism and the Congressional Medal of Honor.

When I drove to Atlanta on the night the Gulf War started, I told myself three things. First, if I didn't know the answer to a question, I would say so. Second, I would reveal no military secrets. Third, I would seek the truth and cling to it faithfully.

A couple of days after the war began, I called James Blackwell on the phone to make contact with my new colleague and discuss how we might support each other during the war. I suggested that we both follow these three basic rules and that, if anyone leaned on us to bend the truth, we would "walk." He readily agreed, and I think we both remained faithful to these basic goals.

Seeking the truth is easy, but finding it in all cases is hard. For instance, as I complete this book, I still do not know whether that first Iraqi target of great controversy was a baby formula factory or a legitimate military target. Preserving classified military information was not difficult. To avoid giving away secrets, I would often ask my Pentagon contacts to help me. If I thought something was on the borderline, I would specifically ask them if I was getting into a classified area. I was pleased that CNN was also sensitive to this problem and would withhold information that they felt might help Saddam Hussein. For instance, CNN never forecast the weather over Iraq for fear the Iraqi military could use the forecast to predict the targets and attack routes of Coalition aircraft and missiles.

There are people reading this book who may think that I am a lackey or an apologist for the Pentagon or that I enhanced the ability of the Pentagon to manage the news and to censor and withhold information that the public had a right to know. I sincerely hope that they are wrong. I tried very hard to inform the public and to encourage decision makers to make enlightened public policy. Six weeks is much too short a time to fully understand CNN, the relationship of the media to the military, and the proper balance between legitimate censorship in warfare and the right to know in a democratic society. However, I would ask all members of the military to view the media not as an enemy, but as an institution of vital importance to the American political culture. In turn, I would ask members of the media to view the military not as a hidebound group of Neanderthals pursuing parochial agendas but as dedicated men and women who are devoting their lives to service to their country. Finally, I would ask viewers of television news to write to the various networks about their concerns so that the networks can be more responsive to these concerns and provide more balanced coverage.

I think that the relationship of the military to the media may have improved as a result of this war. However, my judgment is not shared by many reporters, especially those who were in Saudi Arabia. Many members of the media feel that the censorship in Saudi Arabia was the worst ever imposed on the press in wartime. Many journalists feel that the press pool system must be abandoned, and some feel that the press should be able to hire its own helicopters and vehicles so they can observe the combat and report back quickly to the people. Many also believe that much of the military censorship had as its goal not the hiding of secrets from the enemy but concealing goofs and trying to make the military look good. These criticisms may be a bit overblown, but reporters have a legitimate reason for being in the combat zone and for reporting as accurately and as quickly as is possible.

This great country needs both a military and a media of competence and high integrity. I have now served in both institutions. For a very long time, I have had high respect for the military profession and its strong institutional commitment to public service, high ethical standards, and the principle of civilian control. At times, my respect for the press has wavered. I have never been disturbed when a member of the media makes an honest mistake, since I also have made many mistakes, especially when dealing with short deadlines. I also realize that no reporter can have sufficient knowledge on all the subjects he or she is reporting on. On occasion, however, I have observed a member of the press so manipulate the facts or edit TV tape as to be guilty of gross violations of integrity. My intense six weeks with CNN has reconfirmed my high regard for those who would seek out important events and report them truthfully. In the winter of 1991, as I watched both the military and the press operate under great pressure, I gained greater respect for both institutions.

APPENDIX 1

Acknowledgments

The people who assisted me during my duty as a military analyst on CNN number in the hundreds. In addition, there were dozens of others who helped me with this book. Here are the names, in random order, of those who were especially helpful during and after the Gulf War.

Rick Smith, Lt. Gen. Jim Clapper, Dr. Wayne Thompson, Dr. James Blackwell, Ed Turner, Gail Evans, Charlie Pixley, Eason Jordan, Tom Johnson, Bob Furnad, Josh Loory, Judy Milestone, Diane Durham, Judy Stewart, Betsy Goldman, Bob Cain, Molly McCoy, Susan Rook, Patrick Greenlaw, Col. Don Price, Dr. Al Pierce, Col. Sam Gardiner, Maj. Gen. Jim Pfautz, Dr. Lewis Sorley, Annette Kennedy, Nelle Murrell, Carol Brinson, Connor Smith, Maj. Gen. Dick Stephenson, Zola Murdock, Mike Klein, Charlie Caudill, Sue Bunda, Scott Woelfel, Simon Vicary, Bobbie Battista, Ralph Wenge, Catherine Crier, Lou Waters, Rick Moore, Donna Kelly, Dave

Michaels, Charles Crawford, Sharyl Attkinson, Jonathan Mann, Bernard Shaw, Lauren Oltarsh, Cory Azumbrado, Jennifer Zeidman, Gail Chalef, Wendy Woodward, Patrick Reap, Jill Neff, Larry King, Tammy Haddad, Deb Murphy, David Talley, Francis West, Lt. Col. Dave Deptula, Lt. Gen. Charles May, Gen. Merrill McPeak, Gen. Lee Butler, Lt. Gen. Bernard Trainor, Gen. Mike Dugan, Col. Trevor Dupuy, Col. Roy Stafford, Col. J. J. Winters, Bob Ewart, Randall Shrock, Bill Donnis, Fritz Heinzen, Brig. Gen. Don Sheppard, Charles Hoff, David Kozak, Robert Wiener, Kelly Mills, Mike Dugan, Mick Trainor, Bill Adler, Lt. Col. Mike Gannon, Bettie Sprigg, Arnold Dupuy, Leroy Suddath, Zeb Bradford, Col. Gary Smith, Roger Sorenson, Jim Warren, John Keeley, Maj. Gen. Richard Hawley, Lt. Col. Walter Kooner, Cathy Geyso, George Thibault, Mark Herman, Ed Hurlick, Stephen Pelletiere, Rod Paschall, Maj. Gen. Paul Cerjan, Mike Freney, Jack Jacobs, Bob Evans, Ainie Hastings, McCoy Smith, Robert Verfurth, Serena Verfurth, Judy Henry, Joan Klunder; Lt. Cols. Ronnie A. Stanfill, Bernard E. "Ben" Harvey, Michael B. Nelson, Mark T. Matthews, Ronald J. Tress, Phillip S. Meilinger, Dale C. Hill, Allan W. Harvey, Richard P. King, Larry D. "Dale" Autry; Majs. Roy Y. "Mack" Sikes, Michael B. Hayes, Allen E. Wickman; Capt. Richard D. "Dan" Taylor; M. Sgt. Burnell Davis; Robin Tanner; Gen. H. Norman Schwarzkopf, Maj. Gen. Buster C. Glosson, John Holliman, Gen. Donald J. Kutyna, Carlos Cervantes, Beverly Dolan, Bob Young. All the fellows, advisors, and staff from Group Nine of the W. K. Kellogg Foundation's National Fellowship Program, especially Jay Labov. For those who assisted me and whom I left off the list, my sincere apologies.

I wish to extend a special thanks to those who helped me with the manuscript for this book. Nelle Murrell, Annette Kennedy, and Carol Brinson who took my dictated words, turned them into text on my computer, and helped me refine the manuscript during nine separate revisions. Gail Evans, Eason Jordan, Judy Milestone, Zola Murdoch, and Simon Vicary of CNN who read selected chapters and made helpful suggestions on everything from technical errors to important material that I had initially left out. My two unnamed contacts in the Pentagon who helped me so much during the war and took the time to read and comment critically on the manuscript. Bob Sorley who carefully copyedited two versions of the manuscript. David Talley and Deb Murphy of CNN and Bettie Sprigg of the Office of the Assistant Secretary of Defense, Public Affairs, for helping me find pictures for this book. Connor Smith who read to me out loud every word and punctuation mark of the galley proofs and made hundreds of suggestions on how to improve the substance, syntax, and flow of the book. Mary Creson who provided helpful suggestions on the galley proofs. Hillel Black, my editor at Birch Lane Press, whose candid and often sharp criticism was both maddening and extremely helpful. Donald J. Davidson, the copy editor from Birch Lane Press whose detailed comments and questions helped improve this book significantly. But finally, I must absolve them all of any responsibility for errors, misjudgments, or misinterpretations. That responsibility rests with me alone.

As I did my research for this book, I decided it was essential to ask specific questions of some of the key players in the Gulf War and at CNN. I want especially to thank the individuals who were most generous of their time and most candid in their answers to my questions. First, military and government officials: Gen. H. Norman Schwarzkopf, Lt. Gen. Jim Clapper, Maj. Gen. Buster Glosson, Col. John Warden, Lt. Col. Dave Deptula, Dr. Wayne Thompson, Lt. Gen. Bernard Trainor, and Gen. Mike Dugan. Second, CNN officials: President Tom Johnson, Executive Vice President Ed Turner, Senior Vice President Bob Furnad, Vice President Gail Evans, Vice President Eason Jordan, Judy Milestone, Diane Durham, Simon Vicary, John Holliman, and Wolf Blitzer.

After reviewing great quantities of TV tape, checking all my notes carefully, calling each member of my wartime brain trust to clarify points, and interviewing the key players listed above, I have run into a number of differences of opinions and recollections. I have used my best judgment in sorting through these differences in my attempt to find the truth of what happened in the Persian Gulf, in the Pentagon, and within CNN during the Gulf War. This was my most difficult task.

For those who may wish to research and write about this extraordinary period, I am happy to volunteer my services. I can be reached at (404) 728–9133. If I do not answer, please leave a message on my answering machine and I will call you back.

APPENDIX 2

Key People at CNN

This appendix lists the key peple at CNN who brought to the world in-depth coverage of the war. It is not a complete list of all CNN employees, and I may inadvertently have left off some important people. For those who should have been listed and are not, my sincere apologies. There is a tendency tomove people around to various jobs. Hence, this list reflects who worked where as Kuwait was recaptured in late February 1991.

PRODUCERS LIST

SUPERVISING PRODUCERS
Mike Klein
Charlie Caudill
Jeff Ofgang
Chet Burgess
Vaughn Morrison
Ed Blair

PRODUCERS
Rena Golden
Charlie Schumacher
Carol Kinstle
Brian Richardson
Kathy Womack
Sid Bedingfield

EXECUTIVE PRODUCERS
David Bernkopf
Sue Bunda
Jerry Krieg
Scott Woelfel
Josh Loory
Steve Gallien
Simon Vicary
Marc Bauer
Suzanne Spurgeon

WRITER/PRODUCERS:
Sam Coley
Clint Deloatch
Ralph Robinson
Jim Jenkins
Van Redmond
Jonathan Mintz
Linda Perry
Chandra Whitt

Carper Dulmage
Mary-Helen Martin
Lisa Poissant
Charlie Coates
Liz Mercure
Bruce Chong
Linda Roth
Mary Gregory
Cathy Iachino
Eric Gershon
Anne Adams
Paul Steinhauser
Carla Schmieder
Natalya Ferguson
Siobann Darrow, Sr.
Nicole Couture
Janice McDonald
Larry Blase
Teya Ryan
Phil Frank

ANCHORS

ATLANTA ANCHORS
Bobbie Battista
Molly McCoy
Mary Anne Loughlin
Bob Cain
Ralph Wenge
Catherine Crier
Don Miller
Lou Waters
Patrick Greenlaw
Rick Moore
Dave Walker
Donna Kelly

Susan Rook
Dave Michaels
Charles Crawford
Sharyl Attkisson
Jonathan Mann
Barry Judge

WASHINGTON ANCHORS
Bernard Shaw
Reid Collins
David French

BOOKERS

Gail Evans, vice president
for network booking
Judy Milestone
Lauren Oltarsh
Cory Azumbrado
Gail Chalef
Patrick Reap

Diane Durham
Judy Stewart
Betsy Goldman
Jennifer Zeidman
Wendy Woodward
Jill Neff

THE NEWSGATHERING TEAM AT CNN

International Desk
Eason Jordan, VP &
Managing Editor
Will King, Director of War
Coverage
Steve Springer, Director of
War Coverage
Jane Maxwell, VP Special
Events
Steve Cassidy, Logistics
Becky Mendenhall, Planning
Desk

Domestic Desk
Earl Casey, VP &
Managing Editor
Paul Varian, Sr. National
Editor
Beverly Broadman,
National Editor
Jim Kemp, Planning Desk
Barbara Frank, Planning
Desk

APPENDIX 3

Military Experts Used by CNN During the Gulf War

CNN called upon a large number of military experts (substantially more than the other networks) to provide analysis, insights, perspective. Most of these individuals had spent a career (twenty to thirty-five years) in the military. However, I have listed a few who, while not career military men, served in key positions in the Pentagon or spent most of their professional lives doing research and writing about the military. Former assistant secretaries of defense Richard Perle, Bing West, and Larry Korb are three examples of the first group, and John Keegan, the distinguished British military historian, is an example of the latter group. Some of these experts were called upon a number of times during the war to provide commentary. For instance, Sam Gardiner, an expert on both war games and the operational level of war, was on camera for CNN seven times during the war.

The number of times military experts offered analysis during the Gulf War on CNN exceeds four hundred. In other words, every day there were approximately ten fresh commentaries by military experts on CNN. Half of these were Blackwell or Smith commentaries, and the other half were provided by this large and knowledgeable group of military experts. On the following list, provided by CNN booking, these military experts are arranged in general order of frequency of appearance.

Perry M. Smith	US Air Force, ret.
James A. Blackwell Jr.	US Army, ret., CSIS
Richard Perle	Former assistant secretary of defense
Samuel B. Gardiner	US Air Force, ret., war game expert
Francis "Bing" West	Former assistant secretary of defense
John Keegan	British military historian
Bard E. O'Neill	National War College, terrorism expert
William J. Taylor Jr.	US Army, ret., CSIS
James Schlesinger	Former secretary of defense
Trevor N. Dupuy	US Army, ret., military historian
Caspar Weinberger	Former secretary of defense
James F. Dunnigan	Military analyst, author
Laurence Korb	Former assistant secretary of defense
Edward N. Luttwak	Author, military history and strategy, CSIS
Alexander M. Haig Jr.	US Army, ret., former secretary of state
William E. Odom	US Army, ret., intelligence expert
Harold S. Brown	Former secretary of defense
Eugene Carroll	US Navy, ret., Center for Defense Information

Render Crayton	US Navy, ret., former POW
Sam Dickens	US Air Force, ret.
Jack Fellows	Former POW, Vietnam
Norman Friedman	Naval consultant
Frank Gaffney	Former Pentagon official
Jack H. Jacobs	US Army, ret., Medal of Honor recipient
Tom Grant	Military analyst
Seth Carus	Iraqi weapons expert
Nick Cook	Aviation editor, *Janes*
Robert Dunn	US Navy, ret., naval aviation expert
Fred Frostic	US Air Force, ret., defense analyst, Rand Corporation
John J. Grace	US Marine Corps, ret.
Frank Haynes	US Marine Corps, ret.
Evan Hultman	US Army, ret.
David Super	Military expert
James McWilliams	US Marine Corps, ret.
Jack Merritt	US Army, ret., Association of the US Army
Donald Rumsfeld	Former secretary of defense
Richard Jupa	Iraqi military expert
George J. Keegan Jr.	US Air Force, ret., intelligence expert
Samuel Lessey	Selective Service expert
Wesley McDonald	US Navy, ret., former commander, Atlantic Command
Robert McFarlane	Former National Security advisor
Edgar O'Ballance	British military expert
David Ochmanek	Military expert, Rand Corporation
Ben Rooney	Former British tank commander
Richard V. Secord	US Air Force, ret., Irangate figure
William E. "Ed" Shirron	Combat expert, National War College

Robert H. Spiro	US Navy, ret.
Wayne Waddell	US Air Force, ret.
Daniel Graham	US Army, ret., space expert
Andrew O'Meara	US Army, ret., tank expert
Zeb B. Bradford Jr.	US Army, ret.
Don Jenson	Coast Guard, oil spill expert
Thomas P. Stafford	US Air Force, ret., former astronaut
James Stockdale	US Navy, ret., former POW
William Beecher	Former assistant secretary of defense
Francis Tusa	Armed Forces Journal International
Kenneth Brower	Fellow, British Military College, Sandhurst
Edward Foster	Defense analyst
Walter Boyne	US Air Force, ret., author
Larry Atkinson	US Marine Corps, ret.
Gary Clark	US military mail expert
Edward Carter	US Navy, ret.
Wilma L. Vaught	US Air Force, ret.
John Gilbert	Former British minister of state, defense
Alan L. Gropman	US Air Force, ret., military historian
Michael Gaesal	US Army, ret.
John C. "Doc" Bahnsen Jr.	US Army, ret., combat expert
Julian Lake	US Navy, ret., electronic warfare
Douglas Teith	Former assistant secretary of defense
Nicholas S. H. Krawciw	US Army, ret.
Howard Teicher	Former staff member, National Security Council
Henry Mustin	US Navy, ret.
Thomas Moorer	Former chairman, Joint Chiefs of Staff

Index

215